HENRY IV PART I

HENRY IV
Part I

William Shakespeare

WORDSWORTH CLASSICS

The paper in this book is produced from pure wood
pulp, without the use of chlorine or any other substance
harmful to the environment. The energy used in its
production consists almost entirely of hydroelectricity
and heat generated from waste materials, thereby
conserving fossil fuels and contributing little to the
greenhouse effect.

This edition published 1994 by
Wordsworth Editions Limited
Cumberland House, Crib Street, Ware,
Hertfordshire SG12 9ET

ISBN 1 85326 214 5

Printed and bound in Denmark by Nørhaven

INTRODUCTION

Henry IV Part I, the first part of an historical trilogy, was written and performed about 1597-98, and Shakespeare drew on Hall and Holinshed's chronicles and Daniel's *The Civil Wars* for the background. Henry Percy, the legendary 'Harry Hotspur' and elder son of the Earl of Northumberland, defeats the rebellious Scots but refuses to surrender his prisoners to the king unless his kinsman, Edmund Mortimer, the prisoner of the Welsh leader Owen Glendower, is ransomed. However, Mortimer is a pretender to the throne of England and Henry refuses to ransom him. The Percy family retaliate by siding with the rebels. Against the backdrop of these political and military manoeuvrings, the king's son and heir, Prince Hal, defies his father and the conventions of the court by keeping company with the outrageous Sir John Falstaff – one of Shakespeare's greatest comic characters – in the low life of the tavern. But Prince Hal, on hearing of the uprising against the king, takes command of part of his father's forces and helps to defeat the rebels at the battle of Shrewsbury (1403) during which he saves his father's life and kills Hotspur.

In *Henry IV Part I* Shakespeare explores the theme of ideal kingship and the conflict that occurs between the office of king as eternal and blessed by God, and the king as a fallible man. The central theme of the play is the search for a worthy man to fill the office of king while satisfying these criteria. Within this theme, the nature of true regal honour is explored through the high life of the king and court, the low life of Falstaff and the tavern, and the bloody realities of the battlefield. Hotspur is the straightforward, honourable but hot-headed archetypal warrior whose primary vices are choler and pride. Falstaff is the anarchic lord of misrule and king of the tavern who offers Hal the temptation that could prevent him attaining high kingly destiny. Henry IV, having taken the throne by violent means, is burdened by blood guilt, and despite his competence as a ruler is therefore without legitimate kingly title in the eyes of God. Prince Hal, having gained experience through the court, tavern and battlefield without compromising his integrity, emerges at the end of the play as the complete prince, the Renaissance ideal.

Details of Shakespeare's early life are scanty. He was the son of a prosperous merchant of Stratford-upon-Avon, and tradition has it that he was born on 23rd April 1564; records show that he was baptised three days later. It is likely that he attended the local grammar school, but he had no university education. Of his early career there is no record, though John Aubrey states that he was, for a time, a country schoolmaster. How he became involved with the stage is equally uncertain, but he was sufficiently established as a playwright by 1592 to be criticised in print. He was a leading member of the Lord Chamberlain's Company, which became the King's Men on the accession of James I in 1603. Shakespeare married Anne Hathaway in 1582, by whom he had two daughters and a son, Hamnet, who died in childhood. Towards the end of his life he loosened his ties with London, and retired to New Place, his substantial property in Stratford that he had bought in 1597. He died on 23rd April 1616 aged 52, and is buried in Holy Trinity Church, Stratford.

Further reading:

C L Barber: Shakespeare's Festive Comedy

R Berman: A Reader's Guide to Shakespeare's Plays 1973

R Ornstein: A Kingdom for a Stage: The Achievement of Shakespeare's History Plays 1978

R B Pierce: Shakespeare's History Plays: The Family and the State 1971

E Tillyard: Shakespeare's History Plays 1944 & 1962

J D Wilson: The Fortune's of Falstaff 1943

HENRY IV PART I

The Scene: England

CHARACTERS IN THE PLAY

KING HENRY *the Fourth*

HENRY, *Prince of Wales* ⎱ *sons to the king*
LORD JOHN *of* LANCASTER ⎰

EARL *of* WESTMORELAND

SIR WALTER BLUNT

THOMAS PERCY, *Earl of Worcester*

HENRY PERCY, *Earl of Northumberland*

HENRY PERCY, *surnamed* HOTSPUR, *his son*

EDMUND MORTIMER, *Earl of March*

RICHARD SCROOP, *Archbishop of York*

ARCHIBALD, *Earl of Douglas*

OWEN GLENDOWER

SIR RICHARD VERNON

SIR MICHAEL, *of the household of the Archbishop of York*

EDWARD POINS, *gentleman-in-waiting to Prince Henry*

SIR JOHN FALSTAFF

GADSHILL

PETO

BARDOLPH

LADY PERCY, *wife to Hotspur, and sister to Mortimer*

LADY MORTIMER, *daughter to Glendower, and wife to Mortimer*

MISTRESS QUICKLY, *hostess of the Boar's Head tavern, Eastcheap*

Lords, Officers, Sheriff, Vintner, Chamberlain, Drawers, two Carriers, Travellers, and Attendants

THE FIRST PART OF THE HISTORY OF HENRY IV

[1. 1.]   *London. The Palace*

*KING HENRY with SIR WALTER BLUNT,
meeting WESTMORELAND and others*

King. So shaken as we are, so wan with care,
Find we a time for frighted peace to pant,
And breathe short-winded accents of new broils
To be commenced in strands afar remote:
No more the thirsty entrance of this soil
Shall daub her lips with her own children's blood,
No more shall trenching war channel her fields,
Nor bruise her flowerets with the arméd hoofs
Of hostile paces: those opposéd eyes,
Which, like the meteors of a troubled heaven,   10
All of one nature, of one substance bred,
Did lately meet in the intestine shock
And furious close of civil butchery,
Shall now, in mutual well-beseeming ranks,
March all one way, and be no more opposed
Against acquaintance, kindred, and allies....
The edge of war, like an ill-sheathéd knife,
No more shall cut his master...Therefore, friends,
As far as to the sepulchre of Christ,
Whose soldier now, under whose blesséd cross   20
We are impresséd and engaged to fight,
Forthwith a power of English shall we levy,
Whose arms were moulded in their mothers' womb
To chase these pagans in those holy fields
Over whose acres walked those blesséd feet

Which fourteen hundred years ago were nailed
For our advantage on the bitter cross....
But this our purpose now is twelve month old,
And bootless 'tis to tell you we will go:
30 Therefore we meet not now. Then let me hear
Of you, my gentle cousin Westmoreland,
What yesternight our council did decree
In forwarding this dear expedience.
    Westmoreland. My liege, this haste was hot
        in question,
And many limits of the charge set down
But yesternight, when all athwart there came
A post from Wales, loaden with heavy news,
Whose worst was that the noble Mortimer,
Leading the men of Herefordshire to fight
40 Against the irregular and wild Glendower,
Was by the rude hands of that Welshman taken,
A thousand of his people butcheréd,
Upon whose dead corpse there was such misuse,
Such beastly shameless transformation,
By those Welshwomen done, as may not be
Without much shame retold or spoken of.
    King. It seems then that the tidings of this broil
Brake off our business for the Holy Land.
    Westmoreland. This matched with other did, my
        gracious lord,
50 For more uneven and unwelcome news
Came from the north, and thus it did import:
On Holy-rood day the gallant Hotspur there,
Young Harry Percy, and brave Archibald,
That ever-valiant and approvéd Scot,
At Holmedon met,
Where they did spend a sad and bloody hour;
As by discharge of their artillery,

And shape of likelihood, the news was told;
For he that brought them, in the very heat
And pride of their contention did take horse,   60
Uncertain of the issue any way.

  King. Here is a dear, a true industrious friend,
Sir Walter Blunt, new lighted from his horse,
Stained with the variation of each soil
Betwixt that Holmedon and this seat of ours;
And he hath brought us smooth and welcome news.
The Earl of Douglas is discomfited,
Ten thousand bold Scots, two and twenty knights,
Balked in their own blood did Sir Walter see
On Holmedon's plains. Of prisoners, Hotspur took   70
Mordake the Earl of Fife, and eldest son
To beaten Douglas, and the Earl of Athol,
Of Murray, Angus, and Menteith...
And is not this an honourable spoil?
A gallant prize? ha, cousin, is it not?

  Westmoreland. In faith,
It is a conquest for a prince to boast of.

  King. Yea, there thou mak'st me sad, and mak'st
        me sin
In envy, that my Lord Northumberland
Should be the father to so blest a son...   80
A son who is the theme of honour's tongue,
Amongst a grove the very straightest plant,
Who is sweet Fortune's minion and her pride,
Whilst I by looking on the praise of him
See riot and dishonour stain the brow
Of my young Harry....O that it could be proved
That some night-tripping fairy had exchanged
In cradle-clothes our children where they lay,
And called mine Percy, his Plantagenet,
Then would I have his Harry, and he mine: 90

But let him from my thoughts....What think you, coz,
Of this young Percy's pride? The prisoners,
Which he in this adventure hath surprised,
To his own use he keeps, and sends me word,
I shall have none but Mordake Earl of Fife.
   Westmoreland. This is his uncle's teaching, this
     is Worcester,
Malevolent to you in all aspects,
Which makes him prune himself, and bristle up
The crest of youth against your dignity.
100 *King.* But I have sent for him to answer this;
And for this cause awhile we must neglect
Our holy purpose to Jerusalem....
Cousin, on Wednesday next our council we
Will hold at Windsor, so inform the lords:
But come yourself with speed to us again,
For more is to be said and to be done
Than out of anger can be utteréd.
   Westmoreland. I will, my liege.   *[Exeunt*

[1. 2.]   *London. A room in the house of the*
                 PRINCE OF WALES

SIR JOHN FALSTAFF *lies snoring upon a bench in a corner. The* PRINCE OF WALES *enters and rouses him*

   Falstaff [*waking*]. Now, Hal, what time of day is it, lad?
   Prince. Thou art so fat-witted with drinking of old sack, and unbuttoning thee after supper, and sleeping upon benches after noon, that thou hast forgotten to demand that truly which thou wouldest truly know. What a devil hast thou to do with the time of the day? Unless hours were cups of sack, and minutes capons, and clocks the tongues of bawds, and dials the signs of leaping-

houses, and the blessed sun himself a fair hot wench in 10
flame-coloured taffeta, I see no reason why thou shouldst
be so superfluous to demand the time of the day.

Falstaff. Indeed, you come near me now, Hal, for
we that take purses go by the moon and the seven stars,
and not by Phœbus, he, 'that wandering knight so
fair'.... And, I prithee, sweet wag, when thou art king,
as God save thy grace—majesty I should say, for grace
thou wilt have none.

Prince. What, none?

Falstaff. No, by my troth, not so much as will serve 20
to be prologue to an egg and butter.

Prince. Well, how then? come, roundly, roundly.

Falstaff. Marry then, sweet wag, when thou art king
let not us that are squires of the night's body be called
thieves of the day's beauty; let us be Diana's foresters,
gentlemen of the shade, minions of the moon, and let
men say we be men of good government, being governed
as the sea is by our noble and chaste mistress the moon,
under whose countenance we steal.

Prince. Thou sayest well, and it holds well too, for 30
the fortune of us that are the moon's men doth ebb and
flow like the sea, being governed as the sea is by the
moon—as for proof now, a purse of gold most reso-
lutely snatched on Monday night and most dissolutely
spent on Tuesday morning, got with swearing 'lay by'
and spent with crying 'bring in'—now in as low an ebb
as the foot of the ladder, and by and by in as high a flow
as the ridge of the gallows.

Falstaff. By the Lord, thou sayst true, lad, and is
not my hostess of the tavern a most sweet wench?   40

Prince. As the honey of Hybla, my old lad of the
castle, and is not a buff jerkin a most sweet robe of
durance?

Falstaff. How now, how now, mad wag? what, in thy quips and thy quiddities? what a plague have I to do with a buff jerkin?

Prince. Why, what a pox have I to do with my hostess of the tavern?

Falstaff. Well, thou hast called her to a reckoning
50 many a time and oft.

Prince. Did I ever call for thee to pay thy part?

Falstaff. No, I'll give thee thy due, thou hast paid all there.

Prince. Yea, and elsewhere, so far as my coin would stretch, and where it would not, I have used my credit.

Falstaff. Yea, and so used it that, were it not here apparent that thou art heir apparent—But, I prithee, sweet wag, shall there be gallows standing in England when thou art king? and resolution thus fubbed as it is
60 with the rusty curb of old father Antic the law? Do not thou, when thou art king, hang a thief.

Prince. No, thou shalt.

Falstaff. Shall I? O rare! By the Lord, I'll be a brave judge!

Prince. Thou judgest false already. I mean, thou shalt have the hanging of the thieves and so become a rare hangman.

Falstaff. Well, Hal, well—and in some sort it jumps with my humour, as well as waiting in the court, I can tell you.
70 *Prince.* For obtaining of suits?

Falstaff. Yea, for obtaining of suits, whereof the hangman hath no lean wardrobe....'Sblood, I am as melancholy as a gib cat or a lugged bear.

Prince. Or an old lion, or a lover's lute.

Falstaff. Yea, or the drone of a Lincolnshire bagpipe.

Prince. What sayest thou to a hare, or the melancholy of Moor-ditch?

Falstaff. Thou hast the most unsavoury similes and art indeed the most comparative, rascalliest, sweet young prince....But, Hal, I prithee, trouble me no 80 more with vanity. I would to God thou and I knew where a commodity of good names were to be bought: an old lord of the council rated me the other day in the street about you, sir, but I marked him not, and yet he talked very wisely, but I regarded him not, and yet he talked wisely and in the street too.

Prince. Thou didst well, for wisdom cries out in the streets, and no man regards it.

Falstaff. O, thou hast damnable iteration, and art indeed able to corrupt a saint: thou hast done much harm 90 upon me, Hal—God forgive thee for it: before I knew thee, Hal, I knew nothing, and now am I, if a man should speak truly, little better than one of the wicked... I must give over this life, and I will give it over: by the Lord, an I do not, I am a villain. I'll be damned for never a king's son in Christendom.

Prince. Where shall we take a purse to-morrow, Jack?

Falstaff. 'Zounds, where thou wilt, lad, I'll make one, an I do not, call me villain and baffle me.

Prince. I see a good amendment of life in thee, 100 from praying to purse-taking.

Falstaff. Why, Hal, 'tis my vocation, Hal, 'tis no sin for a man to labour in his vocation.

POINS enters

Poins! Now shall we know if Gadshill have set a match. [*points*] O, if men were to be saved by merit, what hole in hell were hot enough for him? This is the most omnipotent villain that ever cried 'Stand' to a true man.

Prince. Good morrow, Ned.

Poins. Good morrow, sweet Hal. What says Monsieur

110 Remorse? What says Sir John Sack and Sugar? Jack,
how agrees the devil and thee about thy soul, that thou
soldest him on Good Friday last, for a cup of Madeira
and a cold capon's leg?

Prince. Sir John stands to his word, the devil shall
have his bargain, for he was never yet a breaker of
proverbs: he will give the devil his due.

Poins. Then art thou damned for keeping thy word
with the devil.

Prince. Else he had been damned for cozening the devil.

120 *Poins.* But, my lads, my lads, to-morrow morning, by
four o'clock, early at Gad's Hill, there are pilgrims going
to Canterbury with rich offerings, and traders riding to
London with fat purses....I have vizards for you all,
you have horses for yourselves, Gadshill lies to-night in
Rochester, I have bespoke supper to-morrow night in
Eastcheap: we may do it as secure as sleep. If you will
go, I will stuff your purses full of crowns; if you will not,
tarry at home and be hanged.

Falstaff. Hear ye, Yedward, if I tarry at home and
130 go not, I'll hang you for going.

Poins. You will, chops?

Falstaff. Hal, wilt thou make one?

Prince. Who, I? rob? I a thief? not I, by my faith.

Falstaff. There's neither honesty, manhood, nor good
fellowship in thee, nor thou cam'st not of the blood
royal, if thou darest not stand for ten shillings.

[*Poins makes signals behind Falstaff's back*

Prince. Well then, once in my days I'll be a madcap.

Falstaff. Why, that's well said.

Prince. Well, come what will, I'll tarry at home.

140 *Falstaff.* By the Lord, I'll be a traitor then, when thou
art king.

Prince. I care not.

Poins. Sir John, I prithee, leave the prince and me alone, I will lay him down such reasons for this adventure that he shall go.

Falstaff. Well, God give thee the spirit of persuasion, and him the ears of profiting, that what thou speakest may move, and what he hears may be believed, that the true prince may (for recreation sake) prove a false thief, for the poor abuses of the time want countenance... 150 Farewell, you shall find me in Eastcheap.

Prince. Farewell, the latter spring! Farewell, Allhallown summer!   [*Falstaff goes*

Poins. Now, my good sweet honey lord, ride with us to-morrow. I have a jest to execute that I cannot manage alone. Falstaff, Bardolph, Peto and Gadshill shall rob those men that we have already waylaid—yourself and I will not be there: and when they have the booty, if you and I do not rob them, cut this head off from my shoulders.   160

Prince. How shall we part with them in setting forth?

Poins. Why, we will set forth before or after them, and appoint them a place of meeting, wherein it is at our pleasure to fail; and then will they adventure upon the exploit themselves, which they shall have no sooner achieved but we'll set upon them.

Prince. Yea, but 'tis like that they will know us by our horses, by our habits, and by every other appointment, to be ourselves.

Poins. Tut! our horses they shall not see, I'll tie them 170 in the wood; our vizards we will change after we leave them; and, sirrah, I have cases of buckram for the nonce, to immask our noted outward garments.

Prince. Yea, but I doubt they will be too hard for us.

Poins. Well, for two of them, I know them to be as true-bred cowards as ever turned back; and for the

third, if he fight longer than he sees reason, I'll forswear
arms. The virtue of this jest will be the incomprehensible
lies that this same fat rogue will tell us when we meet at
180 supper, how thirty at least he fought with, what wards,
what blows, what extremities he endured, and in the
reproof of this lives the jest.

Prince. Well, I'll go with thee. Provide us all things
necessary, and meet me to-morrow night in Eastcheap,
there I'll sup...Farewell.

Poins. Farewell, my lord.   [*Poins goes*

Prince. I know you all, and will awhile uphold
The unyoked humour of your idleness.
Yet herein will I imitate the sun,
190 Who doth permit the base contagious clouds
To smother up his beauty from the world,
That when he please again to be himself,
Being wanted he may be more wond'red at,
By breaking through the foul and ugly mists
Of vapours that did seem to strangle him.
If all the year were playing holidays,
To sport would be as tedious as to work;
But when they seldom come, they wished for come,
And nothing pleaseth but rare accidents:
200 So, when this loose behaviour I throw off,
And pay the debt I never promiséd,
By how much better than my word I am,
By so much shall I falsify men's hopes,
And like bright metal on a sullen ground,
My reformation, glitt'ring o'er my fault,
Shall show more goodly, and attract more eyes,
Than that which hath no foil to set it off.
I'll so offend, to make offence a skill,
Redeeming time when men think least I will.   [*he goes*

[1. 3.]   *Windsor. The Council Chamber*

Enter the KING, NORTHUMBERLAND, WORCESTER,
HOTSPUR, SIR WALTER BLUNT, *with others*

King. My blood hath been too cold and temperate,
Unapt to stir at these indignities,
And you have found me—for accordingly
You tread upon my patience. But be sure
I will from henceforth rather be myself,
Mighty and to be feared, than my condition,
Which hath been smooth as oil, soft as young down,
And therefore lost that title of respect
Which the proud soul ne'er pays but to the proud.
    Worcester. Our house, my sovereign liege,   10
        little deserves
The scourge of greatness to be used on it,
And that same greatness too which our own hands
Have holp to make so portly.
    Northumberland. My lord,—
    King. Worcester, get thee gone, for I do see
Danger and disobedience in thine eye:
O, sir, your presence is too bold and peremptory,
And majesty might never yet endure
The moody frontier of a servant brow.
You have good leave to leave us. When we need   20
Your use and counsel, we shall send for you....
                      [Worcester goes out
You were about to speak.
    Northumberland. [*bows*]   Yea, my good lord.
Those prisoners in your highness' name demanded,
Which Harry Percy here at Holmedon took,
Were, as he says, not with such strength denied
As is delivered to your majesty.

Either envy, therefore, or misprision
Is guilty of this fault, and not my son.
    Hotspur. My liege, I did deny no prisoners,
30 But I remember, when the fight was done,
When I was dry with rage and extreme toil,
Breathless and faint, leaning upon my sword,
Came there a certain lord, neat and trimly dressed,
Fresh as a bridegroom, and his chin new reaped
Showed like a stubble-land at harvest-home.
He was perfuméd like a milliner,
And 'twixt his finger and his thumb he held
A pouncet-box, which ever and anon
He gave his nose and took't away again—
40 Who therewith angry, when it next came there,
Took it in snuff—and still he smiled and talked:
And as the soldiers bore dead bodies by,
He called them untaught knaves, unmannerly,
To bring a slovenly unhandsome corse
Betwixt the wind and his nobility:
With many holiday and lady terms
He questioned me, amongst the rest demanded
My prisoners in your majesty's behalf.
I then, all smarting with my wounds being cold,
50 To be so pest'red with a popinjay,
Out of my grief and my impatience,
Answered neglectingly I know not what,
He should, or he should not, for he made me mad
To see him shine so brisk, and smell so sweet,
And talk so like a waiting-gentlewoman
Of guns, and drums, and wounds, God save the mark!
And telling me the sovereignest thing on earth
Was parmaceti for an inward bruise,
And that it was great pity, so it was,
60 This villainous salt-petre should be digged

Out of the bowels of the harmless earth,
Which many a good tall fellow had destroyed
So cowardly, and but for these vile guns
He would himself have been a soldier....
This bald unjointed chat of his, my lord,
I answered indirectly, as I said,
And I beseech you, let not his report
Come current for an accusation
Betwixt my love and your high majesty.

Blunt. The circumstance considered, good my lord,   70
Whate'er Lord Harry Percy then had said
To such a person, and in such a place,
At such a time, with all the rest retold,
May reasonably die, and never rise
To do him wrong, or any way impeach
What then he said, so he unsay it now.

King. Why, yet he doth deny his prisoners,
But with proviso and exception,
That we at our own charge shall ransom straight
His brother-in-law, the foolish Mortimer,   80
Who, on my soul, hath wilfully betrayed
The lives of those that he did lead to fight
Against the great magician, damned Glendower,
Whose daughter, as we hear, that Earl of March
Hath lately married...Shall our coffers then
Be emptied to redeem a traitor home?
Shall we buy treason? and indent with fears,
When they have lost and forfeited themselves?
No, on the barren mountains let him starve;
For I shall never hold that man my friend,   90
Whose tongue shall ask me for one penny cost
To ransom home revolted Mortimer.

Hotspur. Revolted Mortimer!
He never did fall off, my sovereign liege,

But by the chance of war. To prove that true
Needs no more but one tongue for all those wounds,
Those mouthéd wounds, which valiantly he took,
When on the gentle Severn's sedgy bank,
In single opposition, hand to hand,
100 He did confound the best part of an hour
In changing hardiment with great Glendower.
Three times they breathed and three times did
    they drink,
Upon agreement, of swift Severn's flood,
Who then affrighted with their bloody looks,
Ran fearfully among the trembling reeds,
And hid his crisp head in the hollow bank
Bloodstainéd with these valiant combatants.
Never did bare and rotten policy
Colour her working with such deadly wounds,
110 Nor never could the noble Mortimer
Receive so many, and all willingly.
Then let him not be slandered with revolt.
   King. Thou dost belie him, Percy, thou dost
    belie him.
He never did encounter with Glendower:
I tell thee,
He durst as well have met the devil alone,
As Owen Glendower for an enemy.
Art thou not ashamed? But, sirrah, henceforth
Let me not hear you speak of Mortimer:
120 Send me your prisoners with the speediest means,
Or you shall hear in such a kind from me
As will displease you....My Lord Northumberland,
We license your departure with your son.
Send us your prisoners, or you'll hear of it.
                [*King Henry, Blunt and other nobles*
                leave the chamber

Hotspur. And if the devil come and roar for them,
I will not send them: I will after straight
And tell him so, for I will ease my heart,
Albeit I make a hazard of my head.
  Northumberland. What, drunk with choler? stay and
     pause awhile,
Here comes your uncle.

Worcester returns

  Hotspur.   Speak of Mortimer!   130
'Zounds, I will speak of him, and let my soul
Want mercy if I do not join with him:
Yea, on his part, I'll empty all these veins,
And shed my dear blood drop by drop in the dust,
But I will lift the down-trod Mortimer
As high in the air as this unthankful king,
As this ingrate and cank'red Bolingbroke.
  Northumberland. Brother, the king hath made your
     nephew mad.
  Worcester. Who struck this heat up after I was gone?
  Hotspur. He will forsooth have all my prisoners,   140
And when I urged the ransom once again
Of my wife's brother, then his cheek looked pale,
And on my face he turned an eye of death,
Trembling even at the name of Mortimer.
  Worcester. I cannot blame him, was not
     he proclaimed,
By Richard that dead is, the next of blood?
  Northumberland. He was, I heard the proclamation:
And then it was when the unhappy king
(Whose wrongs in us God pardon!) did set forth
Upon his Irish expedition;   150
From whence he intercepted did return
To be deposed and shortly murdéred.

Worcester. And for whose death we in the world's
    wide mouth
Live scandalized and foully spoken of.
  Hotspur. But soft, I pray you, did King Richard then
Proclaim my brother Edmund Mortimer
Heir to the crown?
  Northumberland.   He did, myself did hear it.
  Hotspur. Nay, then I cannot blame his cousin king,
That wished him on the barren mountains starve.
160 But shall it be that you, that set the crown
Upon the head of this forgetful man,
And for his sake wear the detested blot
Of murderous subornation, shall it be
That you a world of curses undergo,
Being the agents, or base second means,
The cords, the ladder, or the hangman rather?—
O, pardon me that I descend so low,
To show the line, and the predicament,
Wherein you range under this subtle king!—
170 Shall it for shame be spoken in these days,
Or fill up chronicles in time to come,
 That men of your nobility and power
Did gage them both in an unjust behalf
(As both of you, God pardon it! have done)
To put down Richard, that sweet lovely rose,
And plant this thorn, this canker, Bolingbroke?
And shall it in more shame be further spoken,
That you are fooled, discarded, and shook off
By him for whom these shames ye underwent?
180 No, yet time serves wherein you may redeem
Your banished honours, and restore yourselves
Into the good thoughts of the world again:
Revenge the jeering and disdained contempt
Of this proud king, who studies day and night

To answer all the debt he owes to you,
Even with the bloody payment of your deaths:
Therefore, I say—
   Worcester.   Peace, cousin, say no more.
And now I will unclasp a secret book,
And to your quick-conceiving discontents
I'll read you matter deep and dangerous,   190
As full of peril and adventurous spirit
As to o'er-walk a current roaring loud
On the unsteadfast footing of a spear.
   Hotspur. If he fall in, good night! or sink or swim.
Send danger from the east unto the west,
So honour cross it from the north to south,
And let them grapple: O, the blood more stirs
To rouse a lion than to start a hare!
   Northumberland. Imagination of some great exploit
Drives him beyond the bounds of patience.   200
   Hotspur. By heaven, methinks it were an easy leap,
To pluck bright honour from the pale-faced moon,
Or dive into the bottom of the deep,
Where fathom-line could never touch the ground,
And pluck up drownéd honour by the locks,
So he that doth redeem her thence might wear
Without corrival all her dignities:
But out upon this half-faced fellowship!
   Worcester. He apprehends a world of figures here,
But not the form of what he should attend.   210
Good cousin, give me audience for a while.
   Hotspur. I cry you mercy.
   Worcester.   Those same noble Scots
That are your prisoners,—
   Hotspur.   I'll keep them all;
By God, he shall not have a Scot of them.
No, if a Scot would save his soul, he shall not.

I'll keep them, by this hand.

 Worcester.   You start away,

And lend no ear unto my purposes...

Those prisoners you shall keep.

 Hotspur.   Nay, I will: that's flat:

He said he would not ransom Mortimer,

220 Forbad my tongue to speak of Mortimer,

But I will find him when he lies asleep,

And in his ear I'll holla 'Mortimer!'

Nay,

I'll have a starling shall be taught to speak

Nothing but 'Mortimer', and give it him

To keep his anger still in motion.

 Worcester. Hear you, cousin, a word.

 Hotspur. All studies here I solemnly defy,

Save how to gall and pinch this Bolingbroke.

230 And that same sword-and-buckler Prince of Wales,

But that I think his father loves him not

And would be glad he met with some mischance,

I would have him poisoned with a pot of ale.

 Worcester. Farewell, kinsman! I'll talk to you

When you are better tempered to attend.

 Northumberland. Why, what a wasp-stung and

   impatient fool

Art thou, to break into this woman's mood,

Tying thine ear to no tongue but thine own!

 Hotspur. Why, look you, I am whipped and scourged

   with rods,

240 Nettled, and stung with pismires, when I hear

Of this vile politician, Bolingbroke.

In Richard's time—what de'ye call the place?—

A plague upon't, it is in Gloucestershire;

'Twas where the madcap duke his uncle kept,

His uncle York—where I first bowed my knee

Unto this king of smiles, this Bolingbroke—
'Sblood! When you and he came back from
  Ravenspurgh—
Northumberland. At Berkeley castle.
Hotspur. You say true.
Why, what a candy deal of courtesy   250
This fawning greyhound then did proffer me!
'Look when his infant fortune came to age',
And, 'gentle Harry Percy', and 'kind cousin':
O, the devil take such cozeners! God forgive me!
Good uncle, tell your tale—I have done.
 Worcester. Nay, if you have not, to it again,
We will stay your leisure.
 Hotspur.   I have done, i'faith.
 Worcester. Then once more to your Scottish prisoners.
Deliver them up without their ransom straight,
And make the Douglas' son your only mean 260
For powers in Scotland, which, for divers reasons
Which I shall send you written, be assured
Will easily be granted. You, my lord,
      [*to Northumberland*
Your son in Scotland being thus employed,
Shall secretly into the bosom creep
Of that same noble prelate, well beloved,
The archbishop.
 Hotspur. Of York, is't not?
 Worcester.   True; who bears hard
His brother's death at Bristow, the Lord Scroop.
I speak not this in estimation,
As what I think might be, but what I know 270
Is ruminated, plotted, and set down,
And only stays but to behold the face
Of that occasion that shall bring it on.
 Hotspur. I smell it. Upon my life, it will do well.

Northumberland. Before the game's afoot thou still
  let'st slip.
Hotspur. Why, it cannot choose but be a noble plot.
And then the power of Scotland and of York,
To join with Mortimer, ha?
Worcester.   And so they shall.
Hotspur. In faith, it is exceedingly well aimed.
280 *Worcester.* And 'tis no little reason bids us speed,
To save our heads by raising of a head,
For, bear ourselves as even as we can,
The king will always think him in our debt,
And think we think ourselves unsatisfied,
Till he hath found a time to pay us home.
And see already how he doth begin
To make us strangers to his looks of love.
 Hotspur. He does, he does, we'll be revenged on him.
 Worcester. Cousin, farewell. No further go in this
290 Than I by letters shall direct your course.
When time is ripe, which will be suddenly,
I'll steal to Glendower and Lord Mortimer,
Where you and Douglas and our powers at once,
As I will fashion it, shall happily meet,
To bear our fortunes in our own strong arms,
Which now we hold at much uncertainty.
 Northumberland. Farewell, good brother, we shall
  thrive, I trust.
 Hotspur. Uncle, adieu: O, let the hours be short,
Till fields, and blows, and groans applaud our sport!
            [they go

[2. 1.]   *An inn yard at Rochester*

'*Enter a Carrier with a lantern in his hand*'

1 *Carrier.* Heigh-ho! An't be not four by the day, I'll be hanged. Charles' wain is over the new chimney, and yet our horse not packed. What, ostler!

Ostler [*sleepily, within*]. Anon, anon.

1 *Carrier.* I prithee, Tom, beat Cut's saddle, put a few flocks in the point, poor jade is wrung in the withers, out of all cess.

'*Enter another Carrier*'

2 *Carrier.* Peas and beans are as dank here as a dog, and that is the next way to give poor jades the bots: this house is turned upside down since Robin Ostler 10 died.

1 *Carrier.* Poor fellow never joyed since the price of oats rose, it was the death of him.

2 *Carrier.* I think this be the most villainous house in all London road for fleas, I am stung like a tench.

1 *Carrier.* Like a tench! by the mass, there is ne'er a king christen could be better bit than I have been since the first cock.

2 *Carrier.* Why, they will allow us ne'er a jordan, and then we leak in your chimney, and your chamber-lye 20 breeds fleas like a loach.

1 *Carrier.* What, ostler! come away, and be hanged, come away.

2 *Carrier.* I have a gammon of bacon, and two razes of ginger, to be delivered as far as Charing-cross.

1 *Carrier.* God's body! the turkeys in my pannier are quite starved....What, ostler! a plague on thee! hast thou never an eye in thy head? canst not hear? An 'twere not as good deed as drink, to break the pate on thee, I am a very villain. Come, and be hanged! hast no faith in thee? 30

Enter GADSHILL

Gadshill. Good morrow, carriers, what's o'clock?

1 *Carrier.* I think it be two o'clock.

Gadshill. I prithee, lend me thy lantern to see my gelding in the stable.

1 *Carrier.* Nay, by God, soft, I know a trick worth two of that, ay, faith!

Gadshill. I pray thee, lend me thine.

2 *Carrier.* Ay, when? canst tell? Lend me thy lantern, quoth-a? marry, I'll see thee hanged first.

40 *Gadshill.* Sirrah carrier, what time do you mean to come to London?

2 *Carrier.* Time enough to go to bed with a candle, I warrant thee. [*aside*] Come, neighbour Mugs, we'll call up the gentlemen. They will along with company, for they have great charge. [*the carriers go within*

Gadshill. What, ho! chamberlain!

Voice from within. At hand, quoth pick-purse.

Gadshill. That's even as fair as—at hand, quoth the chamberlain: for thou variest no more from picking of 50 purses than giving direction doth from labouring; thou layest the plot how.

A Chamberlain comes from the inn

Chamberlain. Good morrow, Master Gadshill. It holds current that I told you yesternight. There's a franklin in the wild of Kent, hath brought three hundred marks with him in gold, I heard him tell it to one of his company last night at supper, a kind of auditor, one that hath abundance of charge too, God knows what. They are up already, and call for eggs and butter. They will away presently.

60 *Gadshill.* Sirrah, if they meet not with Saint Nicholas' clerks, I'll give thee this neck.

Chamberlain. No, I'll none of it. I pray thee, keep that for the hangman, for I know thou worshippest Saint Nicholas, as truly as a man of falsehood may.

Gadshill. What talkest thou to me of the hangman? if I hang, I'll make a fat pair of gallows: for, if I hang, old Sir John hangs with me, and thou knowest he's no starveling. Tut! there are other Trojans that thou dream'st not of, the which for sport sake are content to do the profession some grace, that would, if matters 70 should be looked into, for their own credit sake make all whole. I am joined with no foot-land-rakers, no long-staff sixpenny strikers, none of these mad mustachio purple-hued malt-worms, but with nobility and tran-quillity, burgomasters and great onyers, such as can hold in, such as will strike sooner than speak, and speak sooner than drink, and drink sooner than pray. And yet, 'zounds, I lie, for they pray continually to their saint, the commonwealth, or rather not pray to her, but prey on her, for they ride up and down on her, and make her 80 their boots.

Chamberlain. What, the commonwealth their boots? will she hold out water in foul way?

Gadshill. She will, she will—Justice hath liquored her: we steal as in a castle, cock-sure: we have the receipt of fern-seed, we walk invisible.

Chamberlain. Nay, by my faith, I think you are more beholding to the night than to fern-seed for your walking invisible.

Gadshill. Give me thy hand, thou shalt have a share 90 in our purchase, as I am a true man.

Chamberlain. Nay, rather let me have it, as you are a false thief.

Gadshill. Go to, 'homo' is a common name to all men: bid the ostler bring my gelding out of the stable. Fare-well, you muddy knave.   [*they go their ways*

[2. 2.] *A narrow lane, near the top of Gad's Hill, some two miles from Rochester; bushes and trees. A dark night*

The PRINCE, PETO *and* BARDOLPH *come up the hill;* POINS *hurrying after*

Poins. Come, shelter, shelter! I have removed Falstaff's horse, and he frets like a gummed velvet.
Prince. Stand close.   [*Poins hides behind a bush*

FALSTAFF comes up, breathless

Falstaff. Poins! Poins, and be hanged! Poins!
Prince. Peace, ye fat-kidneyed rascal! what a brawling dost thou keep!
Falstaff. Where's Poins, Hal?
Prince. He is walked up to the top of the hill, I'll go seek him.   [*he joins Poins*
10 *Falstaff.* I am accursed to rob in that thief's company. The rascal hath removed my horse, and tied him I know not where. If I travel but four foot by the squier further afoot, I shall break my wind....Well, I doubt not but to die a fair death for all this, if I 'scape hanging for killing that rogue. I have forsworn his company hourly any time this two and twenty years, and yet I am bewitched with the rogue's company. If the rascal have not given me medicines to make me love him, I'll be hanged. It could not be else—I have drunk medicines. Poins! Hal!
20 a plague upon you both! Bardolph! Peto! I'll starve ere I'll rob a foot further. An 'twere not as good a deed as drink, to turn true man and to leave these rogues, I am the veriest varlet that ever chewed with a tooth...Eight yards of uneven ground is threescore and ten miles afoot with me, and the stony-hearted villains know it well enough. A plague upon't, when thieves cannot be

true one to another! ['*they whistle*'.] Whew! A plague
upon you all! Give me my horse, you rogues, give me
my horse and be hanged.

Prince [*coming forward*]. Peace, ye fat-guts! lie down, 30
lay thine ear close to the ground and list if thou canst hear
the tread of travellers.

Falstaff. Have you any levers to lift me up again, being
down? 'Sblood, I'll not bear mine own flesh so far
afoot again for all the coin in thy father's exchequer.
What a plague mean ye to colt me thus?

Prince. Thou liest, thou art not colted, thou art un-
colted.

Falstaff. I prithee, good Prince Hal, help me to my
horse, good king's son.   40

Prince. Out, ye rogue! shall I be your ostler?

Falstaff. Go hang thyself in thine own heir-apparent
garters! If I be ta'en, I'll peach for this...An I have not
ballads made on you all and sung to filthy tunes, let a
cup of sack be my poison—when a jest is so forward, and
afoot too! I hate it.

> GADSHILL *approaches, coming down the hill*

Gadshill. Stand!
Falstaff. So I do, against my will.

> POINS, BARDOLPH, *and* PETO *come forward*

Poins. O, 'tis our setter. I know his voice.
Bardolph. What news?   50
Gadshill. Case ye, case ye, on with your vizards,
there's money of the king's coming down the hill, 'tis
going to the king's exchequer.

Falstaff. You lie, ye rogue, 'tis going to the king's
tavern.

Gadshill. There's enough to make us all.

Falstaff. —To be hanged.

Prince. Sirs, you four shall front them in the narrow
lane: Ned Poins and I will walk lower. If they 'scape
60 from your encounter, then they light on us.

Peto. How many be there of them?

Gadshill. Some eight, or ten.

Falstaff. 'Zounds, will they not rob us?

Prince. What, a coward, Sir John Paunch?

Falstaff. Indeed, I am not John of Gaunt, your grandfather, but yet no coward, Hal.

Prince. Well, we leave that to the proof.

Poins. Sirrah Jack, thy horse stands behind the hedge,
when thou need'st him, there thou shalt find him...Fare-
70 well, and stand fast.

Falstaff. Now cannot I strike him, if I should be
hanged.

(*Prince.* Ned, where are our disguises?

(*Poins.* Here, hard by, stand close.

[*The Prince and Poins slip away*

Falstaff. Now, my masters, happy man be his dole!
say I; every man to his business.

The Travellers are heard coming down the hill

1 *Traveller.* Come, neighbour, the boy shall lead our
horses down the hill, we'll walk afoot awhile and ease
our legs.

80 *Thieves.* Stand!

Travellers. Jesus bless us!

Falstaff. Strike, down with them, cut the villains'
throats! Ah, whoreson caterpillars! bacon-fed knaves!
they hate us youth. Down with them, fleece them.

1 *Traveller.* O, we are undone, both we and ours for
ever.

Falstaff. Hang ye, gorbellied knaves, are ye undone?
No, ye fat chuffs. I would your store were here! On,

bacons, on! What, ye knaves? young men must live. You are grandjurors, are ye? We'll jure ye, faith.   90

[*'Here they rob them and bind them' and then drive them down the hill*

The PRINCE *and* POINS *steal from the bushes disguised in buckram*

Prince. The thieves have bound the true men. Now could thou and I rob the thieves, and go merrily to London, it would be argument for a week, laughter for a month, and a good jest for ever.

Poins. Stand close, I hear them coming.

The Thieves return

Falstaff. Come, my masters, let us share, and then to horse before day. An the Prince and Poins be not two arrant cowards, there's no equity stirring. There's no more valour in that Poins than in a wild-duck.

[*'As they are sharing, the Prince and Poins set upon them'*

Prince. Your money!   100
Poins. Villains!

[*' They all run away, leaving the booty behind them, and Falstaff, after a blow or two, runs away too', roaring for mercy as the Prince and Poins prick him from behind with their swords*

Prince. Got with much ease. Now merrily to horse: the thieves are all scattered, and possessed with fear so strongly that they dare not meet each other. Each takes his fellow for an officer. Away, good Ned. Falstaff sweats to death, and lards the lean earth as he walks along. Were't not for laughing, I should pity him.

Poins. How the fat rogue roared!   [*they go*

[2. 3.] *A room in Warkworth Castle*

'*Enter* HOTSPUR, *solus, reading a letter*'
and striding to and fro

Hotspur. 'But, for mine own part, my lord, I could
be well contented to be there, in respect of the love I
bear your house.'
He could be contented: why is he not then? In
respect of the love he bears our house: he shows in this,
he loves his own barn better than he loves our house.
Let me see some more.
'The purpose you undertake is dangerous.'
Why, that's certain. 'Tis dangerous to take a cold, to
10 sleep, to drink, but I tell you, my lord fool, out of this
nettle, danger, we pluck this flower, safety.
'The purpose you undertake is dangerous, the
friends you have named uncertain, the time itself
unsorted, and your whole plot too light for the counter-
poise of so great an opposition.'
Say you so, say you so? I say unto you again, you are
a shallow cowardly hind, and you lie...What a lack-
brain is this! By the Lord, our plot is a good plot as ever
was laid, our friends true and constant: a good plot, good
20 friends, and full of expectation: an excellent plot, very
good friends...What a frosty-spirited rogue is this! Why,
my lord of York commends the plot and the general
course of the action. 'Zounds, an I were now by this
rascal, I could brain him with his lady's fan. Is there
not my father, my uncle, and myself? Lord Edmund
Mortimer, my lord of York, and Owen Glendower?
is there not besides the Douglas? have I not all their
letters to meet me in arms by the ninth of the next month?
and are they not some of them set forward already?
30 What a pagan rascal is this! an infidel! Ha! you shall
see now, in very sincerity of fear and cold heart, will he

to the king, and lay open all our proceedings! O, I could divide myself and go to buffets, for moving such a dish of skim milk with so honourable an action! Hang him! let him tell the king, we are prepared: I will set forward to-night.

'*Enter his Lady*'

How now, Kate? I must leave you within these two hours.

  Lady Percy. O my good lord, why are you thus alone?
For what offence have I this fortnight been
A banished woman from my Harry's bed?   40
Tell me, sweet lord, what is't that takes from thee
Thy stomach, pleasure, and thy golden sleep?
Why dost thou bend thine eyes upon the earth,
And start so often when thou sit'st alone?
Why hast thou lost the fresh blood in thy cheeks,
And given my treasures and my rights of thee
To thick-eyed musing and curst melancholy?
In thy faint slumbers I by thee have watched,
And heard thee murmur tales of iron wars,
Speak terms of manage to thy bounding steed,   50
Cry 'Courage! to the field!' And thou hast talked
Of sallies and retires, of trenches, tents,
Of palisadoes, frontiers, parapets,
Of basilisks, of cannon, culverin,
Of prisoners' ransom, and of soldiers slain,
And all the currents of a heady fight.
Thy spirit within thee hath been so at war,
And thus hath so bestirred thee in thy sleep,
That beads of sweat have stood upon thy brow,   60
Like bubbles in a late-disturbèd stream,
And in thy face strange motions have appeared,
Such as we see when men restrain their breath

On some great sudden hest. O, what portents are these?
Some heavy business hath my lord in hand,
And I must know it, else he loves me not.
Hotspur. What, ho!

A servant enters

               Is Gilliams with the packet gone?
Servant. He is, my lord, an hour ago.
Hotspur Hath Butler brought those horses from
    the sheriff?
70 *Servant.* One horse, my lord, he brought even now.
Hotspur. What horse? a roan, a crop-ear, is it not?
Servant. It is, my lord.
Hotspur. [*rapt*]   That roan shall be my throne.
Well, I will back him straight: O esperance!
Bid Butler lead him forth into the park.
                      [*the servant goes*
Lady Percy. But hear you, my lord.
Hotspur. What say'st thou, my lady?
Lady Percy. What is it carries you away?
Hotspur. Why, my horse, my love, my horse.
Lady Percy. Out, you mad-headed ape!
80 A weasel hath not such a deal of spleen
As you are tossed with. In faith,
I'll know your business, Harry, that I will.
I fear my brother Mortimer doth stir
About his title, and hath sent for you
To line his enterprize. But if you go—
Hotspur. So far afoot, I shall be weary, love.
Lady Percy. Come, come, you paraquito, answer me
Directly unto this question that I ask.
In faith, I'll break thy little finger, Harry,
90 An if thou wilt not tell me all things true.
Hotspur. Away,

Away, you trifler! Love! I love thee not,
I care not for thee, Kate. This is no world
To play with mammets and to tilt with lips.
We must have bloody noses and cracked crowns,
And pass them current too....God's me, my horse!
What say'st thou, Kate? what wouldst thou have
        with me?
    Lady Percy. Do you not love me? do you not, indeed?
Well, do not then, for since you love me not
I will not love myself. Do you not love me?   100
Nay, tell me if you speak in jest or no.
    Hotspur. Come, wilt thou see me ride?
And when I am a-horseback, I will swear
I love thee infinitely. But hark you, Kate,
I must not have you henceforth question me
Whither I go, nor reason whereabout.
Whither I must, I must. And, to conclude,
This evening must I leave you, gentle Kate.
I know you wise, but yet no farther wise
Than Harry Percy's wife; constant you are,   110
But yet a woman, and for secrecy,
No lady closer, for I well believe
Thou wilt not utter what thou dost not know.
And so far will I trust thee, gentle Kate!
    Lady Percy. How! so far?
    Hotspur. Not an inch further. But hark you, Kate,
Whither I go, thither shall you go too:
To-day will I set forth, to-morrow you—
Will this content you, Kate?
    Lady Percy.   It must, of force.
            [*he hurries forth; she follows, musing*

[2. 4.] *A room at the Boar's Head Tavern in Eastcheap;*
at the back a great fireplace with a settle. Midnight

The PRINCE *enters at one door, crosses the room,*
opens a door opposite, and calls

Prince. Ned, prithee, come out of that fat room, and
lend me thy hand to laugh a little.

Poins. Where hast been, Hal?   [*comes forth*

Prince. With three or four loggerheads, amongst three
or four score hogsheads. I have sounded the very base-
string of humility. Sirrah, I am sworn brother to a leash
of drawers, and can call them all by their christen names,
as Tom, Dick, and Francis. They take it already upon
their salvation, that though I be but Prince of Wales, yet
10 I am the king of Courtesy, and tell me flatly I am no
proud Jack like Falstaff, but a Corinthian, a lad of
mettle, a good boy (by the Lord, so they call me!) and
when I am king of England, I shall command all the
good lads in Eastcheap. They call drinking deep 'dyeing
scarlet', and when you breathe in your watering, they
cry 'hem!' and bid you 'play it off'. To conclude, I am
so good a proficient in one quarter of an hour, that I can
drink with any tinker in his own language during my
life. I tell thee, Ned, thou hast lost much honour, that
20 thou wert not with me in this action...But, sweet Ned—
to sweeten which name of Ned, I give thee this pennyworth of sugar, clapped even now into my hand by an
underskinker, one that never spake other English in his
life than 'Eight shillings and sixpence', and 'You are
welcome', with this shrill addition, 'Anon, anon, sir!
Score a pint of bastard in the Half-moon', or so. But,
Ned, to drive away the time till Falstaff come, I prithee,
do thou stand in some by-room, while I question my
puny drawer to what end he gave me the sugar, and do

thou never leave calling 'Francis', that his tale to me 30
may be nothing but 'Anon'. Step aside, and I'll show
thee a precedent.

*Poins returns to the room whence he came, leaving
the door open behind him*

Poins [*calls*]. Francis!
Prince. Thou art perfect.
Poins. Francis!

Francis bustles in through the other door

Francis. Anon, anon, sir.   [*turns back*
Look down into the Pomgarnet, Ralph.
Prince. Come hither, Francis.
Francis. My lord?
Prince. How long hast thou to serve, Francis?   40
Francis. Forsooth, five years, and as much as to—
Poins [*within*]. Francis!
Francis. Anon, anon, sir.
Prince. Five year! by'r lady, a long lease for the clink-
ing of pewter...But, Francis, darest thou be so valiant
as to play the coward with thy indenture and show it a
fair pair of heels and run from it?
Francis. O Lord, sir! I'll be sworn upon all the books
in England, I could find in my heart—
Poins [*within*]. Francis!   50
Francis. Anon, sir.
Prince. How old art thou, Francis?
Francis. Let me see—about Michaelmas next I shall
be—
Poins [*within*]. Francis!
Francis. Anon, sir. Pray stay a little, my lord.
                    [*he makes toward the by-room*

Prince [*checks him*]. Nay, but hark you, Francis. For the sugar thou gavest me—'twas a pennyworth, was't not?

Francis. O Lord, I would it had been two!

60 *Prince*. I will give thee for it a thousand pound. Ask me when thou wilt, and thou shalt have it—

Poins [*within*]. Francis!

Francis. Anon, anon.

Prince. Anon, Francis? No, Francis, but to-morrow, Francis; or, Francis, a-Thursday; or, indeed, Francis, when thou wilt. But, Francis!

Francis. My lord?

Prince. Wilt thou rob this leathern jerkin, crystal-button, not-pated, agate-ring, puke-stocking, caddis-

70 garter, smooth-tongue, Spanish-pouch,—

Francis. O Lord, sir, who do you mean?

Prince. Why then, your brown bastard is your only drink! for, look you, Francis, your white canvas doublet will sully. In Barbary, sir, it cannot come to so much.

Francis. What, sir?

Poins [*within*]. Francis!

Prince. Away, you rogue, dost thou not hear them call?
[*'Here they both call him; the drawer stands amazed, not knowing which way to go'*

The VINTNER *comes in*

Vintner. What! stand'st thou still, and hear'st such a calling? Look to the guests within. [*Francis goes.*] My

80 lord, old Sir John, with half-a-dozen more, are at the door. Shall I let them in?

Prince. Let them alone awhile, and then open the door. [*Vintner goes.*] Poins!

Poins [*returning*]. Anon, anon, sir.

Prince. Sirrah, Falstaff and the rest of the thieves are at the door. Shall we be merry?

Poins. As merry as crickets, my lad. But hark ye, what cunning match have you made with this jest of the drawer? come, what's the issue?

Prince. I am now of all humours that have showed 90 themselves humours since the old days of goodman Adam to the pupil age of this present twelve o'clock at midnight. [*Francis hurries past carrying drink.*] What's o'clock, Francis?

Francis. Anon, anon, sir.   [*he goes out*

Prince. That ever this fellow should have fewer words than a parrot, and yet the son of a woman! His industry is up-stairs and down-stairs, his eloquence the parcel of a reckoning.... I am not yet of Percy's mind, the Hotspur of the north, he that kills me some six or seven dozen of 100 Scots at a breakfast, washes his hands, and says to his wife, 'Fie upon this quiet life! I want work.' 'O my sweet Harry,' says she, 'how many hast thou killed to-day?' 'Give my roan horse a drench', says he, and answers, 'Some fourteen', an hour after; 'a trifle, a trifle.' I prithee, call in Falstaff. I'll play Percy, and that damned brawn shall play Dame Mortimer his wife. 'Rivo!' says the drunkard: call in Ribs, call in Tallow.

FALSTAFF enters with GADSHILL, BARDOLPH and
PETO; FRANCIS follows with cups of sack
FALSTAFF, taking no heed of PRINCE and POINS,
sits wearily at a table

Poins. Welcome, Jack. Where hast thou been?

Falstaff [*to himself*]. A plague of all cowards, I say, 110 and a vengeance too! marry, and amen! Give me a cup of sack, boy. Ere I lead this life long, I'll sew nether-stocks, and mend them, and foot them too. A plague of

all cowards! Give me a cup of sack, rogue. Is there
no virtue extant?   ['*he drinketh*'

Prince [*points*]. Didst thou never see Titan kiss a dish
of butter (pitiful-hearted Titan!) that melted at the sweet
tale of the sun's? If thou didst, then behold that com-
pound.

120 *Falstaff* [*giving Francis the empty cup*]. You rogue,
here's lime in this sack too...There is nothing but roguery
to be found in villainous man, yet a coward is worse than a
cup of sack with lime in it. A villainous coward! Go thy
ways, old Jack, die when thou wilt. If manhood, good
manhood, be not forgot upon the face of the earth, then
am I a shotten herring...There lives not three good men
unhanged in England, and one of them is fat, and grows
old. God help the while! a bad world, I say. I would
I were a weaver—I could sing psalms or any thing. A
130 plague of all cowards, I say still.

Prince. How now, wool-sack! what mutter you?

Falstaff [*rounds upon him*]. A king's son! If I do not
beat thee out of thy kingdom with a dagger of lath, and
drive all thy subjects afore thee like a flock of wild-
geese, I'll never wear hair on my face more. You, Prince
of Wales!

Prince. Why, you whoreson round man! what's the
matter?

Falstaff. Are not you a coward? answer me to that—
140 and Poins there?

Poins. 'Zounds, ye fat paunch, an ye call me coward,
by the Lord I'll stab thee.   [*he draws his dagger*

Falstaff. I call thee coward! I'll see thee damned ere
I call thee coward—but I would give a thousand pound
I could run as fast as thou canst. You are straight enough
in the shoulders, you care not who sees your back: call
you that backing of your friends? A plague upon such

backing! give me them that will face me. [*to Francis*]
Give me a cup of sack—I am a rogue, if I drunk to-day.

Prince. O villain! thy lips are scarce wiped since thou   150
drunk'st last.

Falstaff. All's one for that. ['*he drinketh*'] A plague
of all cowards, still say I.

Prince. What's the matter?

Falstaff. What's the matter? there be four of us here
have ta'en a thousand pound this day morning.

Prince. Where is it, Jack? where is it?

Falstaff. Where is it? taken from us it is: a hundred
upon poor four of us.

Prince. What, a hundred, man?   160

Falstaff. I am a rogue, if I were not at half-sword with
a dozen of them two hours together. I have 'scaped by
miracle. I am eight times thrust through the doublet,
four through the hose, my buckler cut through and
through, my sword hacked like a handsaw, ecce signum!
[*he draws it*] I never dealt better since I was a man: all
would not do. A plague of all cowards! Let them speak.
If they speak more or less than truth, they are villains
and the sons of darkness.

Prince. Speak, sirs, how was it?   170

Gadshill. We four set upon some dozen—

Falstaff. Sixteen at least, my lord.

Gadshill. And bound them.

Peto. No, no, they were not bound.

Falstaff. You rogue, they were bound, every man of
them, or I am a Jew else, an Ebrew Jew.

Gadshill. As we were sharing, some six or seven fresh
men set upon us—

Falstaff. And unbound the rest, and then come in the
other.   180

Prince. What, fought you with them all?

Falstaff. All! I know not what you call all, but if I fought not with fifty of them I am a bunch of radish: if there were not two or three and fifty upon poor old Jack, then am I no two-legged creature.

Prince. Pray God you have not murdered some of them.

Falstaff. Nay, that's past praying for. I have peppered two of them. Two I am sure I have paid, two rogues in 190 buckram suits...I tell thee what, Hal, if I tell thee a lie, spit in my face, call me horse. Thou knowest my old ward: here I lay, and thus I bore my point. Four rogues in buckram let drive at me—

Prince. What, four? thou said'st but two even now.

Falstaff. Four, Hal, I told thee four.

Poins. Ay, ay, he said four.

Falstaff. These four came all afront, and mainly thrust at me. I made me no more ado, but took all their seven points in my target, thus.

200 *Prince.* Seven? why, there were but four even now.

Falstaff. In buckram?

Poins. Ay, four, in buckram suits.

Falstaff. Seven, by these hilts, or I am a villain else.

(*Prince.* Prithee, let him alone, we shall have more anon.

Falstaff. Dost thou hear me, Hal?

Prince. Ay, and mark thee too, Jack.

Falstaff. Do so, for it is worth the listening to. These nine in buckram that I told thee of—

210 (*Prince.* So, two more already.

Falstaff. Their points being broken—

Poins. Down fell their hose.

Falstaff. Began to give me ground: but I followed me close, came in foot and hand, and with a thought, seven of the eleven I paid.

(*Prince.* O monstrous! eleven buckram men grown out of two!

Falstaff. But, as the devil would have it, three mis-begotten knaves in Kendal green came at my back, and let drive at me, for it was so dark, Hal, that thou couldest 220 not see thy hand.

Prince. These lies are like their father that begets them, gross as a mountain, open, palpable. Why, thou clay-brained guts, thou knotty-pated fool, thou whoreson, obscene, greasy tallow-catch—

Falstaff. What, art thou mad? art thou mad? is not the truth the truth?

Prince. Why, how couldst thou know these men in Kendal green, when it was so dark thou couldst not see thy hand? come tell us your reason. What sayest thou 230 to this?

Poins. Come, your reason, Jack, your reason.

Falstaff. What, upon compulsion? 'Zounds, an I were at the strappado, or all the racks in the world, I would not tell you on compulsion. Give you a reason on compulsion! if reasons were as plentiful as black-berries, I would give no man a reason upon com-pulsion, I.

Prince. I'll be no longer guilty of this sin. [*points*] This sanguine coward, this bed-presser, this horseback- 240 breaker, this huge hill of flesh—

Falstaff. 'Sblood, you starveling, you†eel-skin, you dried neat's-tongue, you bull's-pizzle, you stock-fish! O, for breath to utter what is like thee! you tailor's-yard, you sheath, you bow-case, you vile standing tuck—

Prince. Well, breathe awhile, and then to it again, and when thou hast tired thyself in base comparisons, hear me speak but this.

Poins. Mark, Jack.

250 *Prince.* We two saw you four set on four, and bound
them and were masters of their wealth: mark now, how
a plain tale shall put you down. Then did we two set on
you four, and with a word, out-faced you from your
prize, and have it, yea, and can show it you here in the
house: and, Falstaff, you carried your guts away as
nimbly, with as quick dexterity, and roared for mercy,
and still run and roared, as ever I heard bull-calf. What
a slave art thou, to hack thy sword as thou hast done,
and then say it was in fight! What trick, what device,
260 what starting-hole, canst thou now find out, to hide thee
from this open and apparent shame?

Poins. Come, let's hear, Jack—what trick hast thou
now?

Falstaff. [*solemnly*] By the Lord, I knew ye as well as
he that made ye....Why, hear you, my masters—was it
for me to kill the heir-apparent? should I turn upon the
true prince? why, thou knowest I am as valiant as Her-
cules: but beware instinct—the lion will not touch the true
prince. Instinct is a great matter—I was now a coward
270 on instinct. I shall think the better of myself and thee
during my life; I for a valiant lion, and thou for a true
prince...But, by the Lord, lads, I am glad you have the
money. [*he dances*] Hostess, clap to the doors. Watch
to-night, pray to-morrow. Gallants, lads, boys, hearts of
gold, all the titles of good fellowship come to you! What,
shall we be merry? shall we have a play extempore?

Prince. Content—and the argument shall be thy running away.

Falstaff. Ah! no more of that, Hal, an thou lovest me.

HOSTESS *enters*

280 *Hostess.* O Jesu, my lord the prince,—

Prince. How now, my lady the hostess! what say'st
thou to me?

Hostess. Marry, my lord, there is a nobleman of the court at door would speak with you: he says he comes from your father.

Prince. Give him as much as will make him a royal man, and send him back again to my mother.

Falstaff. What manner of man is he?

Hostess. An old man.

Falstaff. What doth gravity out of his bed at midnight? 290 Shall I give him his answer?

Prince. Prithee, do, Jack.

Falstaff. Faith, and I'll send him packing. [*he goes out*

Prince. Now, sirs! By'r lady, you fought fair, so did you, Peto, so did you, Bardolph. You are lions too, you ran away upon instinct, you will not touch the true prince, no, fie!

Bardolph. Faith, I ran when I saw others run.

Prince. Faith, tell me now in earnest, how came Falstaff's sword so hacked?   300

Peto. Why, he hacked it with his dagger, and said he would swear truth out of England but he would make you believe it was done in fight, and persuaded us to do the like.

Bardolph. Yea, and to tickle our noses with spear-grass to make them bleed, and then to beslubber our garments with it, and swear it was the blood of true men. I did that I did not this seven year before, I blushed to hear his monstrous devices.

Prince. O villain, thou stolest a cup of sack eighteen 310 years ago, and wert taken with the manner, and ever since thou hast blushed extempore. Thou hadst fire and sword on thy side, and yet thou ran'st away. What instinct hadst thou for it?

Bardolph [*thrusts forward his face*]. My lord, do you see these meteors? do you behold these exhalations?

Prince. I do.

Bardolph. What think you they portend?

Prince. Hot livers, and cold purses.

320 *Bardolph.* Choler, my lord, if rightly taken.

Prince. No, if rightly taken, halter.

FALSTAFF returns

Here comes lean Jack, here comes bare-bone: how now, my sweet creature of bombast? how long is't ago, Jack, since thou sawest thine own knee?

Falstaff. My own knee! when I was about thy years, Hal, I was not an eagle's talon in the waist, I could have crept into any alderman's thumb-ring: a plague of sighing and grief! it blows a man up like a bladder. There's villainous news abroad. Here was Sir John Bracy from

330 your father: you must to the court in the morning. That same mad fellow of the north, Percy, and he of Wales, that gave Amaimon the bastinado, and made Lucifer cuckold, and swore the devil his true liegeman upon the cross of a Welsh hook...what a plague call you him?

Poins. Owen Glendower.

Falstaff. Owen, Owen, the same—and his son-in-law, Mortimer, and old Northumberland, and that sprightly Scot of Scots, Douglas, that runs a-horseback up a hill perpendicular—

340 *Prince.* He that rides at high speed, and with his pistol kills a sparrow flying.

Falstaff. You have hit it.

Prince. So did he never the sparrow.

Falstaff. Well, that rascal hath good mettle in him, he will not run.

Prince. Why, what a rascal art thou then, to praise him so for running.

Falstaff. A-horseback, ye cuckoo, but afoot he will not budge a foot.

Prince. Yes, Jack, upon instinct.   350

Falstaff. I grant ye, upon instinct...Well, he is there too, and one Mordake, and a thousand blue-caps more. Worcester is stolen away to-night, thy father's beard is turned white with the news, you may buy land now as cheap as stinking mackerel.

Prince. Why then, it is like, if there come a hot June, and this civil buffeting hold, we shall buy maidenheads as they buy hob-nails, by the hundreds.

Falstaff. By the mass, lad, thou sayest true, it is like we shall have good trading that way...But, tell me, Hal, 360 art not thou horrible afeard? thou being heir-apparent, could the world pick thee out three such enemies again, as that fiend Douglas, that spirit Percy, and that devil Glendower? art thou not horribly afraid? doth not thy blood thrill at it?

Prince. Not a whit, i'faith, I lack some of thy instinct.

Falstaff. Well, thou wilt be horribly chid to-morrow when thou comest to thy father. If thou love me, practise an answer.

Prince. Do thou stand for my father, and examine me 370 upon the particulars of my life.

Falstaff. Shall I? content. This chair shall be my state, this dagger my sceptre, and this cushion my crown.

Prince. Thy state is taken for a joined-stool, thy golden sceptre for a leaden dagger, and thy precious rich crown for a pitiful bald crown!

Falstaff. Well, an the fire of grace be not quite out of thee, now shalt thou be moved. Give me a cup of sack to make my eyes look red, that it may be thought I have wept—for I must speak in passion, and I will do it in 380 King Cambyses' vein.

Prince [*bows*]. Well, here is my leg.

Falstaff. And here is my speech....Stand aside, nobility.

Hostess. O Jesu, this is excellent sport, i'faith.

Falstaff. Weep not, sweet queen, for trickling tears
are vain.

Hostess. O, the father, how he holds his countenance!

Falstaff. For God's sake, lords, convey my tristful
queen,

For tears do stop the flood-gates of her eyes.

Hostess. O Jesu, he doth it as like one of these harlotry
390 players as ever I see!

Falstaff. Peace, good pint-pot, peace, good tickle-
brain.

Harry, I do not only marvel where thou spendest thy
time, but also how thou art accompanied: for though the
camomile, the more it is trodden on the faster it grows,
yet youth, the more it is wasted the sooner it wears...That
thou art my son, I have partly thy mother's word, partly
my own opinion, but chiefly a villainous trick of thine
eye, and a foolish hanging of thy nether lip, that doth
400 warrant me. If then thou be son to me, here lies the
point—why, being son to me, art thou so pointed at?
Shall the blessed sun of heaven prove a micher and eat
blackberries? a question not to be asked. Shall the son
of England prove a thief and take purses? a question to
be asked. There is a thing, Harry, which thou hast often
heard of, and it is known to many in our land by the
name of pitch: this pitch (as ancient writers do report)
doth defile, so doth the company thou keepest: for,
Harry, now I do not speak to thee in drink, but in tears;
410 not in pleasure, but in passion; not in words only, but in
woes also: and yet there is a virtuous man whom I have
often noted in thy company, but I know not his name.

Prince. What manner of man, an it like your majesty?

Falstaff. A goodly portly man, i'faith, and a corpulent,
of a cheerful look, a pleasing eye, and a most noble

carriage, and as I think his age some fifty, or by'r lady
inclining to threescore. And now I remember me, his
name is Falstaff. If that man should be lewdly given,
he deceiveth me; for, Harry, I see virtue in his looks. If
then the tree may be known by the fruit, as the fruit by 420
the tree, then, peremptorily I speak it, there is virtue in
that Falstaff—him keep with, the rest banish. And tell
me now, thou naughty varlet, tell me, where hast thou
been this month?

Prince. Dost thou speak like a king? Do thou stand
for me, and I'll play my father.

Falstaff. Depose me? if thou dost it half so gravely,
so majestically, both in word and matter, hang me up by
the heels for a rabbit-sucker, or a poulter's hare.

> [*they change places*

Prince. Well, here I am set.   430

Falstaff. And here I stand—judge, my masters.

Prince. Now, Harry, whence come you?

Falstaff. My noble lord, from Eastcheap.

Prince. The complaints I hear of thee are grievous.

Falstaff. 'Sblood, my lord, they are false: [*aside*]
nay, I'll tickle ye for a young prince, i'faith.

Prince. Swearest thou, ungracious boy? henceforth
ne'er look on me. Thou art violently carried away from
grace, there is a devil haunts thee in the likeness of an
old fat man, a tun of man is thy companion: why dost 440
thou converse with that trunk of humours, that bolting-
hutch of beastliness, that swollen parcel of dropsies, that
huge bombard of sack, that stuffed cloak-bag of guts,
that roasted Manningtree ox with the pudding in his
belly, that reverend vice, that grey iniquity, that father
ruffian, that vanity in years? Wherein is he good, but to
taste sack and drink it? wherein neat and cleanly, but to
carve a capon and eat it? wherein cunning, but in craft?

wherein crafty, but in villainy? wherein villainous, but
450 in all things? wherein worthy, but in nothing?

Falstaff. I would your grace would take me with you.
Whom means your grace?

Prince. That villainous abominable misleader of
youth, Falstaff, that old white-bearded Satan.

Falstaff. My lord, the man I know.

Prince. I know thou dost.

Falstaff. But to say I know more harm in him than in
myself, were to say more than I know: that he is old,
the more the pity, his white hairs do witness it, but that
460 he is, saving your reverence, a whoremaster, that I
utterly deny: if sack and sugar be a fault, God help the
wicked! if to be old and merry be a sin, then many an
old host that I know is damned: if to be fat be to be
hated, then Pharaoh's lean kine are to be loved. No,
my good lord—banish Peto, banish Bardolph, banish
Poins, but for sweet Jack Falstaff, kind Jack Falstaff,
true Jack Falstaff, valiant Jack Falstaff, and therefore
more valiant being as he is old Jack Falstaff, banish not
him thy Harry's company, banish not him thy Harry's
470 company, banish plump Jack, and banish all the world.

Prince. I do, I will.

'Enter BARDOLPH, running'

Bardolph. O, my lord, my lord, the sheriff with a most
monstrous watch is at the door!

Falstaff. Out, ye rogue! play out the play. I have
much to say in the behalf of that Falstaff.

'Enter the Hostess'

Hostess. O Jesu, my lord, my lord!—

Prince. Heigh, heigh! the devil rides upon a fiddle-
stick. What's the matter?

Hostess. The sheriff and all the watch are at the door, they are come to search the house, shall I let them in? 480

Falstaff. Dost thou hear, Hal? never call a true piece of gold a counterfeit. Thou art essentially made, without seeming so.

Prince. And thou a natural coward, without instinct.

Falstaff. I deny your major, if you will deny the sheriff, so, if not, let him enter. If I become not a cart as well as another man, a plague on my bringing up! I hope I shall as soon be strangled with a halter as another.

Prince. Go, hide thee behind the arras, the rest walk 490 up above. Now, my masters, for a true face and good conscience.

Falstaff. Both which I have had, but their date is out, and therefore I'll hide me.

           [he does so; all but the Prince and Poins
                                  go out

Prince. Call in the sheriff.—

           '*Enter Sheriff and the Carrier*'

Now, master sheriff, what is your will with me?

Sheriff. First, pardon me, my lord. A hue and cry Hath followed certain men unto this house.

Prince. What men?

Sheriff. One of them is well known, my gracious lord, 500 A gross fat man.

Carrier. As fat as butter.

Prince. The man, I do assure you, is not here, For I myself at this time have employed him: And, sheriff, I will engage my word to thee That I will by to-morrow dinner-time Send him to answer thee, or any man,

For any thing he shall be charged withal.
And so let me entreat you leave the house.

510 *Sheriff.* I will, my lord...There are two gentlemen
Have in this robbery lost three hundred marks.

Prince. It may be so: if he have robbed these men,
He shall be answerable—and so, farewell.

Sheriff. Good night, my noble lord.

Prince. I think it is good morrow, is it not?

Sheriff. Indeed, my lord, I think it be two o'clock.

> [*Sheriff and Carrier depart*

Prince. This oily rascal is known as well as Paul's...
Go, call him forth.

Poins. [*lifts the arras*] Falstaff! fast asleep behind the
520 arras, and snorting like a horse.

Prince. Hark, how hard he fetches breath. Search
his pockets. ['*He searcheth his pocket, and findeth
certain papers*'] What hast thou found?

Poins. Nothing but papers, my lord.

Prince. Let's see what they be—read them.

Poins. Item, A capon	.	.	.	.	2*s.* 2*d.*
Item, Sauce	.	.	.	.	.	4*d.*
Item, Sack, two gallons	.	.	.	5*s.* 8*d.*
Item, Anchovies and sack after supper	.	.	2*s.* 6*d.*
530 Item, Bread	.	.	.	.	.	.	ob.

Prince. O monstrous! but one half-pennyworth of
bread to this intolerable deal of sack! What there is else
keep close, we'll read it at more advantage; there let him
sleep till day. I'll to the court in the morning. We must
all to the wars, and thy place shall be honourable. I'll
procure this fat rogue a charge of foot, and I know his
death will be a march of twelve-score. The money shall
be paid back again with advantage.... Be with me betimes
in the morning, and so good morrow, Poins.

540 *Poins.* Good morrow, good my lord.   [*they go*

[3. 1.]   *Wales. A room in Glendower's house*

'Enter HOTSPUR, WORCESTER, LORD MORTIMER,
and OWEN GLENDOWER', *carrying papers*

Mortimer. These promises are fair, the parties sure,
And our induction full of prosperous hope.

Hotspur. Lord Mortimer, and cousin Glendower, will
you sit down? and uncle Worcester: a plague upon it,
I have forgot the map!

Glendower. No, here it is...Sit cousin Percy, sit good
cousin Hotspur, for by that name as oft as Lancaster doth
speak of you, his cheek looks pale, and with a rising sigh
he wisheth you in heaven.   [*they sit*

Hotspur. And you in hell, as oft as he hears Owen 10
Glendower spoke of.

Glendower. I cannot blame him: at my nativity
The front of heaven was full of fiery shapes,
Of burning cressets, and at my birth
The frame and huge foundation of the earth
Shaked like a coward.

Hotspur. Why, so it would have done at the same
season, if your mother's cat had but kittened, though
yourself had never been born.

Glendower. I say the earth did shake, when I was born. 20

Hotspur. And I say the earth was not of my mind,
If you suppose as fearing you it shook.

Glendower. The heavens were all on fire, the earth
        did tremble.

Hotspur. O, then the earth shook to see the heavens
        on fire,
And not in fear of your nativity.
Diseaséd nature oftentimes breaks forth
In strange eruptions; oft the teeming earth

Is with a kind of colic pinched and vexed
By the imprisoning of unruly wind
30 Within her womb, which for enlargement striving
Shakes the old beldam earth, and topples down
Steeples and moss-grown towers. At your birth
Our grandam earth, having this distemperature,
In passion shook.

   Glendower.   Cousin, of many men
I do not bear these crossings. Give me leave
To tell you once again that at my birth
The front of heaven was full of fiery shapes,
The goats ran from the mountains, and the herds
Were strangely clamorous to the frighted fields.
40 These signs have marked me extraordinary,
And all the courses of my life do show
I am not in the roll of common men...
Where is he living, clipped in with the sea
That chides the banks of England, Scotland, Wales,
Which calls me pupil or hath read to me?
And bring him out that is but woman's son
Can trace me in the tedious ways of art,
And hold me pace in deep experiments.

   Hotspur. I think there's no man speaks better Welsh:
50 I'll to dinner.   [*he rises*

   (*Mortimer.* Peace, cousin Percy, you will make
      him mad.

   Glendower. I can call spirits from the vasty deep.

   Hotspur. Why, so can I, or so can any man,
But will they come when you do call for them?

   Glendower. Why, I can teach you, cousin, to
      command the devil.

   Hotspur. And I can teach thee, coz, to shame the devil,
By telling truth. Tell truth and shame the devil...
If thou have power to raise him, bring him hither,

And I'll be sworn I have power to shame him hence:
O, while you live, tell truth and shame the devil.   60
  Mortimer. Come, come, no more of this unprofitable
    chat.
  Glendower. Three times hath Henry Bolingbroke
    made head
Against my power—thrice from the banks of Wye
And sandy-bottomed Severn have I sent him
Bootless home and weather-beaten back.
  Hotspur. Home without boots, and in foul weather too!
How 'scapes he agues, in the devil's name?
  Glendower. Come, here's the map, shall we divide
    our right,
According to our threefold order ta'en?
                   [*the map is spread upon the table*
  Mortimer. The archdeacon hath divided it   70
Into three limits, very equally:
England, from Trent to Severn hitherto,
By south and east is to my part assigned:
All westward, Wales beyond the Severn shore,
And all the fertile land within that bound,
To Owen Glendower: and, dear coz, to you
The remnant northward, lying off from Trent.
And our indentures tripartite are drawn,
Which being sealéd interchangeably,
(A business that this night may execute)   80
To-morrow, cousin Percy, you and I
And my good Lord of Worcester will set forth
To meet your father and the Scottish power,
As is appointed us, at Shrewsbury.
My father Glendower is not ready yet,
Nor shall we need his help these fourteen days.
[*to Glendower*] Within that space you may have
    drawn together

Your tenants, friends, and neighbouring gentlemen.

   Glendower. A shorter time shall send me to you, lords,

90 And in my conduct shall your ladies come,

From whom you now must steal and take no leave,

For there will be a world of water shed

Upon the parting of your wives and you.

   Hotspur [*studying the map*]. Methinks, my moiety,
     north from Burton here,

In quantity equals not one of yours.

See how this river comes me cranking in,

And cuts me from the best of all my land

A huge half-moon, a monstrous cantle out.

I'll have the current in this place dammed up,

100 And here the smug and silver Trent shall run

In a new channel, fair and evenly.

It shall not wind with such a deep indent,

To rob me of so rich a bottom here.

   Glendower. Not wind? it shall, it must—you see, it doth.

   Mortimer. Yea, but

Mark how he bears his course, and runs me up

With like advantage on the other side,

Gelding the opposéd continent as much

As on the other side it takes from you.

110 *Worcester.* Yea, but a little charge will trench him here,

And on this north side win this cape of land,

And then he runs straight and even.

   Hotspur. I'll have it so, a little charge will do it.

   Glendower. I'll not have it altered.

   Hotspur.   Will not you?

   Glendower. No, nor you shall not.

   Hotspur.   Who shall say me nay?

   Glendower. Why, that will I.

   Hotspur. Let me not understand you then, speak it in Welsh.

Glendower. I can speak English, lord, as well as you,
For I was trained up in the English court, 120
Where being but young I framéd to the harp
Many an English ditty, lovely well,
And gave the tongue a helpful ornament,
A virtue that was never seen in you.

Hotspur. Marry,
And I am glad of it with all my heart!
I had rather be a kitten and cry mew
Than one of these same metre ballad-mongers—
I had rather hear a brazen canstick turned,
Or a dry wheel grate on the axle-tree, 130
And that would set my teeth nothing on edge,
Nothing so much as mincing poetry—
'Tis like the forced gait of a shuffling nag.

Glendower. Come, you shall have Trent turned.

Hotspur. I do not care, I'll give thrice so much land
To any well-deserving friend:
But in the way of bargain, mark ye me,
I'll cavil on the ninth part of a hair.
Are the indentures drawn? shall we be gone?

Glendower. The moon shines fair, you may away 140
    by night:
I'll haste the writer, and withal
Break with your wives of your departure hence.
I am afraid my daughter will run mad,
So much she doteth on her Mortimer.   [*he goes out*

Mortimer. Fie, cousin Percy! how you cross
    my father!

Hotspur. I cannot choose. Sometime he angers me
With telling me of the moldwarp and the ant,
Of the dreamer Merlin and his prophecies,
And of a dragon and a finless fish,
A clip-winged griffin and a moulten raven, 150

A couching lion and a ramping cat,
And such a deal of skimble-skamble stuff
As puts me from my faith. I tell you what—
He held me last night at least nine hours
In reckoning up the several devils' names
That were his lackeys. I cried, 'hum', and 'well,
    go to',
But marked him not a word. O, he is as tedious
As a tired horse, a railing wife,
Worse than a smoky house—I had rather live
160 With cheese and garlic in a windmill, far,
Than feed on cates and have him talk to me
In any summer house in Christendom.
  Mortimer. In faith, he is a worthy gentleman,
Exceedingly well read, and profited
In strange concealments, valiant as a lion,
And wondrous affable, and as bountiful
As mines of India...Shall I tell you, cousin?
He holds your temper in a high respect,
And curbs himself even of his natural scope,
170 When you come 'cross his humour, faith, he does.
I warrant you, that man is not alive
Might so have tempted him as you have done,
Without the taste of danger and reproof—
But do not use it oft, let me entreat you.
  Worcester. In faith, my lord, you are too wilful blame,
And since your coming hither have done enough
To put him quite beside his patience.
You must needs learn, lord, to amend this fault.
Though sometimes it show greatness, courage, blood—
180 And that's the dearest grace it renders you—
Yet oftentimes it doth present harsh rage,
Defect of manners, want of government,
Pride, haughtiness, opinion, and disdain,

The least of which haunting a nobleman
Loseth men's hearts, and leaves behind a stain
Upon the beauty of all parts besides,
Beguiling them of commendation.

　Hotspur. Well, I am schooled—good manners be
　　your speed!
Here come our wives, and let us take our leave.

　　　　'Enter GLENDOWER with the LADIES'

　Mortimer. This is the deadly spite that angers me—　190
My wife can speak no English, I no Welsh.

　Glendower. My daughter weeps, she'll not part
　　with you,
She'll be a soldier too, she'll to the wars.

　Mortimer. Good father, tell her that she and my
　　aunt Percy
Shall follow in your conduct speedily.

　　　　*'Glendower speaks to her in Welsh, and she
　　　　　answers him in the same'*

　Glendower. She is desperate here, a peevish self-willed
harlotry, one that no persuasion can do good upon.

　　　　She turns to Mortimer and 'speaks in Welsh'

　Mortimer. I understand thy looks. That pretty Welsh
Which thou pourest down from these swelling heavens
I am too perfect in, and but for shame　　　200
In such a parley should I answer thee.

　　　　'The lady' speaks 'again in Welsh'

I understand thy kisses and thou mine,
And that's a feeling disputation,
But I will never be a truant, love,
Till I have learned thy language, for thy tongue
Makes Welsh as sweet as ditties highly penned,
Sung by a fair queen in a summer's bower,
With ravishing division, to her lute.

Glendower. Nay, if you melt, then will she run mad.

'*The lady speaks again in Welsh*'

210 *Mortimer.* O, I am ignorance itself in this!

Glendower. She bids you on the wanton rushes lay
    you down,
And rest your gentle head upon her lap,
And she will sing the song that pleaseth you,
And on your eyelids crown the god of sleep,
Charming your blood with pleasing heaviness,
Making such difference 'twixt wake and sleep
As is the difference betwixt day and night,
The hour before the heavenly-harnessed team
Begins his golden progress in the east.

220 *Mortimer.* With all my heart I'll sit and hear her sing,
By that time will our book, I think, be drawn.

Glendower. Do so,   [*Mortimer sits, and she with him*
And those musicians that shall play to you
Hang in the air a thousand leagues from hence,
And straight they shall be here. Sit and attend.

Hotspur. Come, Kate, thou art perfect in lying down.
Come, quick, quick, that I may lay my head in thy lap.

Lady Percy. Go, ye giddy goose.

[*he catches her by the wrist; she struggles; they
sit upon the rushes, he with his head in her lap;
'the music plays*'

Hotspur. Now I perceive the devil understands Welsh,
230 And 'tis no marvel, he is so humorous.
By'r lady, he is a good musician.

Lady Percy. Then should you be nothing but musical,
for you are altogether governed by humours. Lie still,
ye thief, and hear the lady sing in Welsh.

Hotspur. I had rather hear Lady, my brach, howl in
Irish.

Lady Percy. Wouldst thou have thy head broken?

Hotspur. No.

Lady Percy. Then be still.

Hotspur. Neither—'tis a woman's fault.   240

Lady Percy. Now God help thee!

Hotspur. To the Welsh lady's bed.

Lady Percy. What's that?

Hotspur. Peace! she sings.

> ['*Here the lady sings a Welsh song*'

Hotspur. Come, Kate, I'll have your song too.

Lady Percy. Not mine, in good sooth.

Hotspur. Not yours, in good sooth! Heart! you swear
like a comfit-maker's wife—'not you, in good sooth',
and 'as true as I live', and 'as God shall mend me', and
'as sure as day'—   250
And givest such sarcenet surety for thy oaths,
As if thou never walk'st further than Finsbury.
Swear me, Kate, like a lady as thou art,
A good mouth-filling oath, and leave 'in sooth',
And such protest of pepper-gingerbread,
To velvet-guards and Sunday citizens.
Come, sing.

Lady Percy. I will not sing.

Hotspur. 'Tis the next way to turn tailor, or be red-
breast teacher. An the indentures be drawn, I'll away 260
within these two hours—and so come in when ye will.

> [*he goes*

Glendower. Come, come, Lord Mortimer, you are
      as slow
As hot Lord Percy is on fire to go.
By this our book is drawn. We'll but seal,
And then to horse immediately.

Mortimer.   With all my heart.

> [*they go*

[3. 2.]   *London. A room in the palace*

'*The* KING, PRINCE *of* WALES, *and others*'

King. Lords, give us leave. The Prince of Wales and I
Must have some private conference. But be near
     at hand,
For we shall presently have need of you....
                   [*Lords withdraw*
I know not whether God will have it so
For some displeasing service I have done,
That, in his secret doom, out of my blood
He'll breed revengement and a scourge for me;
But thou dost in thy passages of life
Make me believe that thou art only marked
10 For the hot vengeance and the rod of heaven,
To punish my mistreadings. Tell me else,
Could such inordinate and low desires,
Such poor, such bare, such lewd, such mean attempts,
Such barren pleasures, rude society,
As thou art matched withal, and grafted to,
Accompany the greatness of thy blood,
And hold their level with thy princely heart?
    Prince. So please your majesty, I would I could
Quit all offences with as clear excuse
20 As well as I am doubtless I can purge
Myself of many I am charged withal.
Yet such extenuation let me beg,
As, in reproof of many tales devised,
Which oft the ear of greatness needs must hear,
By smiling pickthanks and base newsmongers,
I may for some things true, wherein my youth
Hath faulty wand'red and irregular,
Find pardon on my true submission.

King. God pardon thee! yet let me wonder, Harry,
At thy affections, which do hold a wing   30
Quite from the flight of all thy ancestors.
Thy place in council thou hast rudely lost,
Which by thy younger brother is supplied,
And art almost an alien to the hearts
Of all the court and princes of my blood.
The hope and expectation of thy time
Is ruined, and the soul of every man
Prophetically do forethink thy fall...
Had I so lavish of my presence been,
So common-hackneyed in the eyes of men,   40
So stale and cheap to vulgar company,
Opinion, that did help me to the crown,
Had still kept loyal to possession,
And left me in reputeless banishment,
A fellow of no mark nor likelihood.
By being seldom seen, I could not stir
But like a comet I was wond'red at;
That men would tell their children 'This is he!'
Others would say 'Where? which is Bolingbroke?'
And then I stole all courtesy from heaven,   50
And dressed myself in such humility
That I did pluck allegiance from men's hearts,
Loud shouts and salutations from their mouths,
Even in the presence of the crownéd king....
Thus did I keep my person fresh and new,
My presence like a robe pontifical,
Ne'er seen but wond'red at, and so my state,
Seldom but sumptuous, showéd like a feast,
And wan by rareness such solemnity....
The skipping king, he ambled up and down   60
With shallow jesters and rash bavin wits,
Soon kindled and soon burnt, carded his state,

Mingled his royalty with cap'ring fools,
Had his great name profanéd with their scorns,
And gave his countenance, against his name,
To laugh at gibing boys, and stand the push
Of every beardless vain comparative,
Grew a companion to the common streets,
Enfeoffed himself to popularity,
70 That, being daily swallowed by men's eyes,
They surfeited with honey and began
To loathe the taste of sweetness, whereof a little
More than a little is by much too much.
So when he had occasion to be seen,
He was but as the cuckoo is in June,
Heard, not regarded; seen, but with such eyes
As, sick and blunted with community,
Afford no extraordinary gaze,
Such as is bent on sun-like majesty,
80 When it shines seldom in admiring eyes;
But rather drowzed and hung their eyelids down,
Slept in his face, and rend'red such aspect
As cloudy men use to their adversaries,
Being with his presence glutted, gorged, and full.
And in that very line, Harry, standest thou,
For thou hast lost thy princely privilege
With vile participation. Not an eye
But is a-weary of thy common sight,
Save mine, which hath desired to see thee more,
90 Which now doth that I would not have it do,
Make blind itself with foolish tenderness.
  Prince. I shall hereafter, my thrice gracious lord,
Be more myself.
  King.   For all the world
As thou art to this hour was Richard then,
When I from France set foot at Ravenspurgh,

And even as I was then is Percy now.
Now by my sceptre and my soul to boot,
He hath more worthy interest to the state
Than thou the shadow of succession.
For of no right, nor colour like to right,   100
He doth fill fields with harness in the realm,
Turns head against the lion's arméd jaws,
And, being no more in debt to years than thou,
Leads ancient lords and reverend bishops on
To bloody battles and to bruising arms.
What never-dying honour hath he got
Against renownéd Douglas! whose high deeds,
Whose hot incursions and great name in arms
Holds from all soldiers chief majority,
And military title capital,   110
Through all the kingdoms that acknowledge Christ.
Thrice hath this Hotspur, Mars in swathling clothes,
This infant warrior, in his enterprizes
Discomfited great Douglas, ta'en him once,
Enlargéd him and made a friend of him,
To fill the mouth of deep defiance up,
And shake the peace and safety of our throne.
And what say you to this? Percy, Northumberland,
The Archbishop's grace of York, Douglas, Mortimer,
Capitulate against us and are up....   120
But wherefore do I tell these news to thee?
Why, Harry, do I tell thee of my foes,
Which art my nearest and dearest enemy?
Thou that art like enough, through vassal fear,
Base inclination and the start of spleen,
To fight against me under Percy's pay,
To dog his heels and curtsy at his frowns,
To show how much thou art degenerate.
 Prince. Do not think so, you shall not find it so;

130 And God forgive them that so much have swayed
Your majesty's good thoughts away from me!
I will redeem all this on Percy's head,
And in the closing of some glorious day
Be bold to tell you that I am your son,
When I will wear a garment all of blood,
And stain my favours in a bloody mask,
Which washed away shall scour my shame with it.
And that shall be the day, whene'er it lights,
That this same child of honour and renown,
140 This gallant Hotspur, this all-praiséd knight,
And your unthought-of Harry chance to meet.
For every honour sitting on his helm
Would they were multitudes, and on my head
My shames redoubled! for the time will come,
That I shall make this northern youth exchange
His glorious deeds for my indignities.
Percy is but my factor, good my lord,
To engross up glorious deeds on my behalf,
And I will call him to so strict account
150 That he shall render every glory up,
Yea, even the slightest worship of his time,
Or I will tear the reckoning from his heart....
This, in the name of God, I promise here,
The which if He be pleased I shall perform,
I do beseech your majesty may salve
The long-grown wounds of my intemperature:
If not, the end of life cancels all bands,
And I will die a hundred thousand deaths
Ere break the smallest parcel of this vow.
160 *King.* A hundred thousand rebels die in this—
Thou shalt have charge and sovereign trust herein.
Enter BLUNT
How now, good Blunt? thy looks are full of speed.

Blunt. So hath the business that I come to speak of.
Lord Mortimer of Scotland hath sent word
That Douglas and the English rebels met
The eleventh of this month at Shrewsbury.
A mighty and a fearful head they are,
If promises be kept on every hand,
As ever off'red foul play in a state.

  King. The Earl of Westmoreland set forth to-day,   170
With him my son, Lord John of Lancaster,
For this advertisement is five days old.
On Wednesday next, Harry, you shall set forward,
On Thursday, we ourselves will march: our meeting
Is Bridgenorth, and, Harry, you shall march
Through Gloucestershire; by which account,
Our business valuéd, some twelve days hence
Our general forces at Bridgenorth shall meet.
Our hands are full of business, let's away,
Advantage feeds him fat while men delay.   *[they go* 180

[3. 3.]   *A room at the Boar's Head Tavern
in Eastcheap; early morning*

Enter FALSTAFF *(a truncheon hanging at his girdle)
and* BARDOLPH

  Falstaff. Bardolph, am I not fallen away vilely since
this last action? do I not bate? do I not dwindle? Why,
my skin hangs about me like an old lady's loose gown, I
am withered like an old apple-John. Well, I'll repent,
and that suddenly, while I am in some liking. I shall be
out of heart shortly, and then I shall have no strength
to repent. An I have not forgotten what the inside of a
church is made of, I am a peppercorn, a brewer's horse.
The inside of a church! Company, villainous company,
hath been the spoil of me.   10

Bardolph. Sir John, you are so fretful you cannot live long.

Falstaff. Why, there is it: come, sing me a bawdy song, make me merry....I was as virtuously given as a gentle-man need to be; virtuous enough, swore little, diced not above seven times a week, went to a bawdy-house not above once in a quarter of an hour, paid money that I borrowed three or four times, lived well, and in good compass: and now I live out of all order, out of all 20 compass.

Bardolph. Why, you are so fat, Sir John, that you must needs be out of all compass; out of all reasonable com-pass, Sir John.

Falstaff. Do thou amend thy face, and I'll amend my life: thou art our admiral, thou bearest the lantern in the poop, but 'tis in the nose of thee: thou art the Knight of the Burning Lamp.

Bardolph. Why, Sir John, my face does you no harm.

Falstaff. No, I'll be sworn—I make as good use of it 30 as many a man doth of a death's-head or a memento mori. I never see thy face but I think upon hell-fire, and Dives that lived in purple; for there he is in his robes, burning, burning. If thou wert any way given to virtue, I would swear by thy face; my oath should be, 'by this fire, that's God's angel'. But thou art altogether given over; and wert indeed, but for the light in thy face, the son of utter darkness. When thou ran'st up Gad's Hill in the night to catch my horse, if I did not think thou hadst been an ignis fatuus or a ball of wildfire, there's no 40 purchase in money. O, thou art a perpetual triumph, an everlasting bonfire-light! Thou hast saved me a thousand marks in links and torches, walking with thee in the night betwixt tavern and tavern: but the sack that thou hast drunk me would have bought me lights as good cheap at the dearest chandler's in Europe. I have maintained that salamander of yours with fire any time this two and thirty years, God reward me for it!

Bardolph. 'Sblood, I would my face were in your belly!

Falstaff. God-a-mercy! so should I be sure to be heart-50 burned.

Hostess *enters*

How now, Dame Partlet the hen! have you inquired yet who picked my pocket?

Hostess. Why, Sir John, what do you think, Sir John? do you think I keep thieves in my house? I have searched, I have inquired, so has my husband, man by man, boy by boy, servant by servant. The tithe of a hair was never lost in my house before.

Falstaff. Ye lie, hostess—Bardolph was shaved, and lost many a hair, and I'll be sworn my pocket was 60 picked: go to, you are a woman, go.

Hostess. Who, I? no, I defy thee: God's light, I was never called so in mine own house before.

Falstaff. Go to, I know you well enough.

Hostess. No, Sir John, you do not know me, Sir John. I know you, Sir John. You owe me money, Sir John, and now you pick a quarrel to beguile me of it. I bought you a dozen of shirts to your back.

Falstaff. Dowlas, filthy dowlas. I have given them away to bakers' wives. They have made bolters of 70 them.

Hostess. Now, as I am a true woman, holland of eight shillings an ell! You owe money here besides, Sir John, for your diet and by-drinkings, and money lent you, four and twenty pound.

Falstaff. He had his part of it, let him pay.

Hostess. He? alas, he is poor, he hath nothing.

Falstaff. How! poor? look upon his face. What call you rich? let them coin his nose, let them coin his cheeks.
80 I'll not pay a denier! What, will you make a younker of me? shall I not take mine ease in mine inn but I shall have my pocket picked? I have lost a seal-ring of my grandfather's worth forty mark.

Hostess. O Jesu! I have heard the prince tell him, I know not how oft, that that ring was copper.

Falstaff. How! the prince is a Jack, a sneak-up. 'Sblood, an he were here, I would cudgel him like a dog, if he would say so.

'Enter the PRINCE' *and* POINS, *'marching', single file;* '*FALSTAFF meets' them 'playing upon his truncheon like a fife.' They march together round the room;* BARDOLPH *falling in beside* POINS.

Falstaff. How now, lad! is the wind in that door,
90 i'faith? must we all march?

Bardolph. Yea, two and two, Newgate fashion.

Hostess. My lord, I pray you, hear me.

Prince. What say'st thou, Mistress Quickly? How doth thy husband? I love him well, he is an honest man.

Hostess. Good my lord, hear me.

Falstaff. Prithee, let her alone, and list to me.

Prince. What say'st thou, Jack?

Falstaff. The other night I fell asleep here, behind the arras, and had my pocket picked. This house is turned
100 bawdy-house, they pick pockets.

Prince. What didst thou lose, Jack?

Falstaff. Wilt thou believe me, Hal? three or four bonds of forty pound a-piece, and a seal-ring of my grandfather's.

Prince. A trifle, some eight-penny matter.

Hostess. So I told him, my lord, and I said I heard your grace say só: and, my lord, he speaks most vilely of you, like a foul-mouthed man as he is, and said he would cudgel you.

Prince. What! he did not?   110

Hostess. There's neither faith, truth, nor womanhood in me else.

Falstaff. There's no more faith in thee than in a stewed prune, nor no more truth in thee than in a drawn fox—and for womanhood, Maid Marian may be the deputy's wife of the ward to thee. Go, you thing, go.

Hostess. Say, what thing? what thing?

Falstaff. What thing? why, a thing to thank God on.

Hostess. I am nothing to thank God on, I would thou shouldst know it. I am an honest man's wife, and setting 120 thy knighthood aside, thou art a knave to call me so.

Falstaff. Setting thy womanhood aside, thou art a beast to say otherwise.

Hostess. Say, what beast, thou knave, thou?

Falstaff. What beast? why, an otter.

Prince. An otter, Sir John! why an otter?

Falstaff. Why? she's neither fish nor flesh, a man knows not where to have her.

Hostess. Thou art an unjust man in saying so, thou or any man knows where to have me, thou knave, thou! 130

Prince. Thou say'st true, hostess, and he slanders thee most grossly.

Hostess. So he doth you, my lord, and said this other day you ought him a thousand pound.

Prince. Sirrah, do I owe you a thousand pound?

Falstaff. A thousand pound, Hal? a million. Thy love is worth a million, thou owest me thy love.

Hostess. Nay, my lord, he called you Jack, and said he would cudgel you.

140 *Falstaff.* Did I, Bardolph?

Bardolph. Indeed, Sir John, you said so.

Falstaff. Yea, if he said my ring was copper.

Prince. I say 'tis copper. Darest thou be as good as thy word now?

Falstaff. Why, Hal, thou knowest, as thou art but man I dare, but as thou art prince I fear thee as I fear the roaring of the lion's whelp.

Prince. And why not as the lion?

Falstaff. The king himself is to be feared as the lion.
150 Dost thou think I'll fear thee as I fear thy father? nay, an I do, I pray God my girdle break.

Prince. O, if it should, how would thy guts fall about thy knees! But, sirrah, there's no room for faith, truth, nor honesty, in this bosom of thine—it is all filled up with guts and midriff. Charge an honest woman with picking thy pocket! why, thou whoreson, impudent, embossed rascal, if there were anything in thy pocket but tavern-reckonings, memorandums of bawdy-houses, and one poor pennyworth of sugar-candy to make thee long-
160 winded—if thy pocket were enriched with any other injuries but these, I am a villain. And yet you will stand to it, you will not pocket up wrong! Art thou not ashamed?

Falstaff. Dost thou hear, Hal? thou knowest in the state of innocency Adam fell, and what should poor Jack Falstaff do in the days of villainy? Thou seest I have more flesh than another man, and therefore more frailty...You confess then, you picked my pocket?

Prince. It appears so by the story.

170 *Falstaff.* Hostess, I forgive thee. Go, make ready breakfast, love thy husband, look to thy servants, cherish thy guests. Thou shalt find me tractable to any honest reason, thou seest I am pacified still. Nay, prithee, be

gone. [*Hostess goes*] Now Hal, to the news at court: for
the robbery, lad, how is that answered?

Prince. O, my sweet beef, I must still be good angel
to thee. The money is paid back again.

Falstaff. O, I do not like that paying back, 'tis a
double labour.

Prince. I am good friends with my father, and may 180
do any thing.

Falstaff. Rob me the exchequer the first thing thou
doest, and do it with unwashed hands too.

Bardolph. Do, my lord.

Prince. I have procured thee, Jack, a charge of foot.

Falstaff. I would it had been of horse. Where shall I
find one that can steal well? O for a fine thief, of the age
of two and twenty or thereabouts! I am heinously un-
provided. Well, God be thanked for these rebels, they
offend none but the virtuous; I laud them, I praise them. 190

Prince. Bardolph—

Bardolph. My lord.

Prince. Go bear this letter to Lord John of Lancaster,
to my brother John, this to my Lord of Westmoreland.
Go, Poins, to horse, to horse, for thou and I
Have thirty miles to ride yet ere dinner time.
Jack, meet me to-morrow in the Temple hall
at two o'clock in the afternoon.
There shalt thou know thy charge, and there receive
Money and order for their furniture.   200
The land is burning, Percy stands on high,
And either we or they must lower lie.

                       [he follows Bardolph and Poins

Falstaff. Rare words! brave world! Hostess, my
    breakfast, come!

O, I could wish this tavern were my drum.   *[he goes*

[4. 1.] *A tent in the rebel camp near Shrewsbury*
HOTSPUR, WORCESTER, *and* DOUGLAS

Hotspur. Well said, my noble Scot! If speaking truth
In this fine age were not thought flattery,
Such attribution should the Douglas have,
As not a soldier of this season's stamp
Should go so general current through the world.
By God, I cannot flatter, I do defy
The tongues of soothers, but a braver place
In my heart's love hath no man than yourself.
Nay, task me to my word, approve me, lord.
10 *Douglas.* Thou art the king of honour.
No man so potent breathes upon the ground
But I will beard him.
   Hotspur.   Do so, and 'tis well.
        '*Enter one with letters*'
What letters hast thou there?—I can but thank you.
  Messenger. These letters come from your father—
  Hotspur. Letters from him! why comes he not himself?
  Messenger. He cannot come, my lord, he is
      grievous sick.
  Hotspur. 'Zounds! how has he the leisure to be sick
In such a justling time? Who leads his power?
Under whose government come they along?
20 *Messenger.* His letters bear his mind, not I, my lord.
  Worcester. I prithee, tell me, doth he keep his bed?
  Messenger. He did, my lord, four days ere I set forth,
And at the time of my departure thence
He was much feared by his physicians.
  Worcester. I would the state of time had first
      been whole,
Ere he by sickness had been visited.
His health was never better worth than now.

Hotspur. Sick now! droop now! this sickness doth infect
The very life-blood of our enterprise,
'Tis catching hither, even to our camp.   30
He writes me here that inward sickness—
And that his friends by deputation could not
So soon be drawn, nor did he think it meet
To lay so dangerous and dear a trust
On any soul removed but on his own.
Yet doth he give us bold advertisement
That with our small conjunction we should on,
To see how fortune is disposed to us.
For as he writes there is no quailing now,
Because the king is certainly possessed   40
Of all our purposes. What say you to it?
  Worcester. Your father's sickness is a maim to us.
  Hotspur. A perilous gash, a very limb lopped off—
And yet, in faith, it is not. His present want
Seems more than we shall find it: were it good
To set the exact wealth of all our states
All at one cast? to set so rich a main
On the nice hazard of one doubtful hour?
It were not good, for therein should we read
The very bottom and the soul of hope,   50
The very list, the very utmost bound
Of all our fortunes.
  Douglas.   Faith, and so we should.
Where now remains a sweet reversion,
We may boldly spend upon the hope of what
Is to come in.
A comfort of retirement lives in this.
  Hotspur. A rendezvous, a home to fly unto,
If that the devil and mischance look big
Upon the maidenhead of our affairs.
  Worcester. But yet I would your father had been here... 60

The quality and hair of our attempt
Brooks no division. It will be thought,
By some that know not why he is away,
That wisdom, loyalty, and mere dislike
Of our proceedings kept the earl from hence.
And think how such an apprehension
May turn the tide of fearful faction,
And breed a kind of question in our cause:
For well you know we of the off'ring side
70 Must keep aloof from strict arbitrement,
And stop all sight-holes, every loop from whence
The eye of reason may pry in upon us.
This absence of your father's draws a curtain
That shows the ignorant a kind of fear
Before not dreamt of.
   Hotspur.   You strain too far.
I rather of his absence make this use—
It lends a lustre and more great opinion,
A larger dare to our great enterprise,
Than if the earl were here; for men must think,
80 If we without his help can make a head
To push against a kingdom, with his help
We shall o'erturn it topsy-turvy down.
Yet all goes well, yet all our joints are whole.
   Douglas. As heart can think. There is not such a word
Spoke of in Scotland as this term of fear.

SIR RICHARD VERNON enters the tent

   Hotspur. My cousin Vernon! welcome, by my soul.
   Vernon. Pray God, my news be worth a welcome, lord.
The Earl of Westmoreland, seven thousand strong,
Is marching hitherwards, with him Prince John.
90 *Hotspur.* No harm—what more?
   Vernon.   And further, I have learned,

The king himself in person is set forth,
Or hitherwards intended speedily,
With strong and mighty preparation.
  Hotspur. He shall be welcome too: where is his son,
The nimble-footed madcap Prince of Wales,
And his comrades, that daffed the world aside,
And bid it pass?
  Vernon.   All furnished, all in arms;
†All plumed like estridges that wing the wind,
Baited like eagles having lately bathed,
Glittering in golden coats like images,   100
As full of spirit as the month of May,
And gorgeous as the sun at midsummer,
Wanton as youthful goats, wild as young bulls.
I saw young Harry with his beaver on,
His cushes on his thighs, gallantly armed,
Rise from the ground like feathered Mercury,
And vaulted with such ease into his seat,
As if an angel dropped down from the clouds,
To turn and wind a fiery Pegasus,
And witch the world with noble horsemanship.   110
  Hotspur. No more, no more! worse than the sun
      in March,
This praise doth nourish agues. Let them come,
They come like sacrifices in their trim,
And to the fire-eyed maid of smoky war
All hot and bleeding will we offer them.
The mailéd Mars shall on his altar sit,
Up to the ears in blood. I am on fire
To hear this rich reprisal is so nigh,
And yet not ours...Come, let me taste my horse,
Who is to bear me like a thunderbolt   120
Against the bosom of the Prince of Wales.
Harry to Harry shall, hot horse to horse,

Meet and ne'er part till one drop down a corse.
O, that Glendower were come!
   Vernon.   There is more news.
I learned in Worcester, as I rode along,
He cannot draw his power this fourteen days.
   Douglas. That's the worst tidings that I hear of yet.
   Worcester. Ay, by my faith, that bears a frosty sound.
   Hotspur. What may the king's whole battle reach unto?
130 *Vernon.* To thirty thousand.
   Hotspur.   Forty let it be!
My father and Glendower being both away,
The powers of us may serve so great a day.
Come, let us take a muster speedily—
Doomsday is near—die all, die merrily.
   Douglas. Talk not of dying, I am out of fear
Of death or death's hand for this one half year.
                    [they hurry from the tent

[4. 2.]   *A highway near Coventry*

Enter FALSTAFF, *in quilted leather jack-coat and with
a pistol-case slung at his belt, talking with* BARDOLPH

   Falstaff. Bardolph, get thee before to Coventry, fill
me a bottle of sack, our soldiers shall march through.
We'll to Sutton Co'fil' to-night. *[he gives him a bottle*
   Bardolph. Will you give me money, captain?
   Falstaff. Lay out, lay out.
   Bardolph. This bottle makes an angel.
   Falstaff. An if it do, take it for thy labour—and if it
make twenty, take them all, I'll answer the coinage.
Bid my lieutenant Peto meet me at town's end.
10 *Bardolph.* I will, captain. Farewell.   *[he goes*
   Falstaff. If I be not ashamed of my soldiers, I am a
soused gurnet. I have misused the king's press damnably.

I have got in exchange of a hundred and fifty soldiers three hundred and odd pounds. I press me none but good householders, yeomen's sons, inquire me out contracted bachelors, such as had been asked twice on the banns, such a commodity of warm slaves, as had as lieve hear the devil as a drum, such as fear the report of a caliver worse than a struck fowl or a hurt wild-duck: I pressed me none but such toasts-and-butter, with hearts 20 in their bellies no bigger than pins' heads, and they have bought out their services, and now my whole charge consists of ancients, corporals, lieutenants, gentlemen of companies—slaves as ragged as Lazarus in the painted cloth, where the Glutton's dogs licked his sores, and such as indeed were never soldiers, but discarded unjust serving-men, younger sons to younger brothers, revolted tapsters, and ostlers trade-fallen, the cankers of a calm world and a long peace, ten times more dishonourable ragged than an old fazed ancient; and 30 such have I to fill up the rooms of them as have bought out their services, that you would think that I had a hundred and fifty tattered prodigals, lately come from swine-keeping, from eating draff and husks. A mad fellow met me on the way, and told me I had unloaded all the gibbets and pressed the dead bodies. No eye hath seen such scarecrows. I'll not march through Coventry with them, that's flat: nay, and the villains march wide betwixt the legs as if they had gyves on, for indeed I had the most of them out of prison. There's 40 not a shirt and a half in all my company, and the half shirt is two napkins tacked together and thrown over the shoulders like a herald's coat without sleeves, and the shirt, to say the truth, stolen from my host at Saint Alban's or the red-nose innkeeper of Daventry. But that's all one; they'll find linen enough on every hedge.

Prince HENRY and WESTMORELAND come up from behind

Prince. How now, blown Jack? how now, quilt?

Falstaff. What, Hal? how now, mad wag? what a devil dost thou in Warwickshire?—My good Lord of 50 Westmoreland, I cry you mercy. I thought your honour had already been at Shrewsbury.

Westmoreland. Faith, Sir John, 'tis more than time that I were there, and you too; but my powers are there already. The king, I can tell you, looks for us all, we must away all night.

Falstaff. Tut, never fear me, I am as vigilant as a cat to steal cream.

Prince. I think, to steal cream indeed, for thy theft hath already made thee butter. But tell me, Jack, whose 60 fellows are these that come after?

Falstaff. Mine, Hal, mine.

Prince. I did never see such pitiful rascals.

Falstaff. Tut, tut, good enough to toss, food for powder, food for powder—they'll fill a pit as well as better; tush, man, mortal men, mortal men.

Westmoreland. Ay, but, Sir John, methinks they are exceeding poor and bare, too beggarly.

Falstaff. Faith, for their poverty, I know not where they had that, and for their bareness I am sure they 70 never learned that of me.

Prince. No, I'll be sworn, unless you call three fingers in the ribs, bare. But, sirrah, make haste. Percy is already in the field. [*he goes*

Falstaff. What, is the king encamped?

Westmoreland. He is, Sir John. I fear we shall stay too long. [*he hurries forward*

Falstaff. Well,
To the latter end of a fray and the beginning of a feast
Fits a dull fighter and a keen guest. [*he follows*

[4. 3.]   *The rebel camp near Shrewsbury*

Enter HOTSPUR, WORCESTER, DOUGLAS, *and*
VERNON

Hotspur. We'll fight with him to-night.
Worcester.   It may not be.
Douglas. You give him then advantage.
Vernon.   Not a whit.
Hotspur. Why say you so? looks he not for supply?
Vernon. So do we.
Hotspur.   His is certain, ours is doubtful.
Worcester. Good cousin, be advised, stir not to-night.
Vernon. Do not, my lord.
Douglas.   You do not counsel well;
You speak it out of fear and cold heart.
Vernon. Do me no slander, Douglas. By my life,
And I dare well maintain it with my life,
If well-respected honour bid me on,   10
I hold as little counsel with weak fear
As you, my lord, or any Scot that this day lives.
Let it be seen to-morrow in the battle,
Which of us fears.
Douglas.   Yea, or to-night.
Vernon.   Content.
Hotspur. To-night, say I.
Vernon. Come, come, it may not be. I wonder much,
Being men of such great leading as you are,
That you foresee not what impediments
Drag back our expedition. Certain horse
Of my cousin Vernon's are not yet come up,   20
Your uncle Worcester's horse came but to-day,
And now their pride and mettle is asleep,
Their courage with hard labour tame and dull,
That not a horse is half the half himself.

Hotspur. So are the horses of the enemy
In general, journey-bated and brought low.
The better part of ours are full of rest.
   Worcester. The number of the king exceedeth ours.
For God's sake, cousin, stay till all come in.
                    [' *the trumpet sounds a parley*'

SIR WALTER BLUNT *comes up*

30 *Blunt.* I come with gracious offers from the king,
If you vouchsafe me hearing and respect.
   Hotspur. Welcome, Sir Walter Blunt; and would
        to God,
You were of our determination!
Some of us love you well, and even those some
Envy your great deservings and good name,
Because you are not of our quality,
But stand against us like an enemy.
   Blunt. And God defend but still I should stand so,
So long as out of limit and true rule
40 You stand against anointed majesty.
But to my charge. The king hath sent to know
The nature of your griefs, and whereupon
You conjure from the breast of civil peace
Such bold hostility, teaching his duteous land
Audacious cruelty. If that the king
Have any way your good deserts forgot,
Which he confesseth to be manifold,
He bids you name your griefs, and with all speed
You shall have your desires with interest,
50 And pardon absolute for yourself and these
Herein misled by your suggestion.
   Hotspur. The king is kind, and well we know the king
Knows at what time to promise, when to pay:
My father and my uncle and myself

Did give him that same royalty he wears:
And when he was not six and twenty strong,
Sick in the world's regard, wretched and low,
A poor unminded outlaw sneaking home,
My father gave him welcome to the shore;
And when he heard him swear and vow to God   60
He came but to be Duke of Lancaster,
To sue his livery and beg his peace
With tears of innocency and terms of zeal,
My father, in kind heart and pity moved,
Swore him assistance and performed it too.
Now when the lords and barons of the realm
Perceived Northumberland did lean to him,
The more and less came in with cap and knee,
Met him in boroughs, cities, villages,
Attended him on bridges, stood in lanes,   70
Laid gifts before him, proffered him their oaths,
Gave him their heirs as pages, followed him
Even at the heels in golden multitudes.
He presently, as greatness knows itself,
Steps me a little higher than his vow
Made to my father while his blood was poor
Upon the naked shore at Ravenspurgh;
And now, forsooth, takes on him to reform
Some certain edicts and some strait decrees
That lie too heavy on the commonwealth,   80
Cries out upon abuses, seems to weep
Over his country wrongs, and by this face,
This seeming brow of justice, did he win
The hearts of all that he did angle for;
Proceeded further—cut me off the heads
Of all the favourites that the absent king
In deputation left behind him here,
When he was personal in the Irish war.

Blunt. Tut, I came not to hear this.

Hotspur.   Then to the point.

90 In short time after he deposed the king,
Soon after that deprived him of his life,
And in the neck of that tasked the whole state;
To make that worse, suffered his kinsman March
(Who is, if every owner were well placed,
Indeed his king) to be engaged in Wales,
There without ransom to lie forfeited;
Disgraced me in my happy victories,
Sought to entrap me by intelligence,
Rated mine uncle from the council-board,
100 In rage dismissed my father from the court,
Broke oath on oath, committed wrong on wrong,
And in conclusion drove us to seek out
This head of safety, and withal to pry
Into his title, the which we find
Too indirect for long continuance.

Blunt. Shall I return this answer to the king?

Hotspur. Not so, Sir Walter. We'll withdraw awhile;
Go to the king, and let there be impawned
Some surety for a safe return again,
110 And in the morning early shall mine uncle
Bring him our purposes—and so farewell.

Blunt. I would you would accept of grace and love.

Hotspur. And may be so we shall.

Blunt.   Pray God you do.

[they withdraw

[4. 4.] *York. A room in the Archbishop's palace*

The ARCHBISHOP of YORK, and SIR MICHAEL

Archbishop. Hie, good Sir Michael, bear this
    sealéd brief
With wingéd haste to the lord marshal,
This to my cousin Scroop, and all the rest
To whom they are directed. If you knew
How much they do import, you would make haste.
  Sir Michael. My good lord,
I guess their tenour.
  Archbishop.   Like enough you do.
To-morrow, good Sir Michael, is a day
Wherein the fortune of ten thousand men
Must bide the touch; for, sir, at Shrewsbury,   10
As I am truly given to understand,
The king with mighty and quick-raiséd power
Meets with Lord Harry: and I fear, Sir Michael,
What with the sickness of Northumberland,
Whose power was in the first proportion,
And what with Owen Glendower's absence thence,
Who with them was a rated sinew too,
And comes not in, o'er-ruled by prophecies,
I fear the power of Percy is too weak
To wage an instant trial with the king.   20
  Sir Michael. Why, my good lord, you need not fear,
There is the Douglas and Lord Mortimer.
  Archbishop. No, Mortimer is not there.
  Sir Michael. But there is Mordake, Vernon, Lord
    Harry Percy,
And there is my Lord of Worcester, and a head
Of gallant warriors, noble gentlemen.
  Archbishop. And so there is: but yet the king hath drawn

The special head of all the land together—
The Prince of Wales, Lord John of Lancaster,
30 The noble Westmoreland and warlike Blunt,
And many moe corrivals and dear men
Of estimation and command in arms.

   Sir Michael. Doubt not, my lord, they shall be
       well opposed.

   Archbishop. I hope no less, yet needful 'tis to fear.
And, to prevent the worst, Sir Michael, speed:
For if Lord Percy thrive not, ere the king
Dismiss his power, he means to visit us,
For he hath heard of our confederacy,
And 'tis but wisdom to make strong against him.
40 Therefore, make haste. I must go write again
To other friends, and so farewell, Sir Michael.

                               [*they go*

[5. 1.]   *The King's camp near Shrewsbury*

Enter the KING, *Prince* HENRY (*his helm fluttering
with ostrich-feathers*), LORD JOHN *of* LANCASTER,
SIR WALTER BLUNT, *and* FALSTAFF

   King. How bloodily the sun begins to peer
Above yon busky hill! the day looks pale
At his distemp'rature.

   Prince.   The southern wind
Doth play the trumpet to his purposes,
And by his hollow whistling in the leaves
Foretells a tempest and a blust'ring day.

   King. Then with the losers let it sympathize,
For nothing can seem foul to those that win.

                        ['*the trumpet sounds*'

Enter WORCESTER *and* VERNON

How now, my Lord of Worcester? 'tis not well

That you and I should meet upon such terms   10
As now we meet. You have deceived our trust,
And made us doff our easy robes of peace,
To crush our old limbs in ungentle steel.
This is not well, my lord, this is not well.
What say you to it? will you again unknit
This churlish knot of all-abhorréd war?
And move in that obedient orb again
Where you did give a fair and natural light,
And be no more an exhaled meteor,
A prodigy of fear, and a portent   20
Of broachéd mischief to the unborn times?
  Worcester. Hear me, my liege:
For mine own part, I could be well content
To entertain the lag-end of my life
With quiet hours; for I do protest
I have not sought the day of this dislikè.
  King. You have not sought it! how comes it then?
  Falstaff. Rebellion lay in his way and he found it.
  Prince. Peace, chewet, peace!
  Worcester. It pleased your majesty to turn your looks 30
Of favour from myself and all our house,
And yet I must remember you, my lord,
We were the first and dearest of your friends.
For you my staff of office did I break
In Richard's time, and posted day and night
To meet you on the way, and kiss your hand,
When yet you were in place and in account
Nothing so strong and fortunate as I.
It was myself, my brother, and his son,
That brought you home, and boldly did outdare   40
The dangers of the time. You swore to us,
And you did swear that oath at Doncaster,
That you did nothing purpose 'gainst the state,

Nor claim no further than your new-fall'n right,
The seat of Gaunt, dukedom of Lancaster:
To this we swore our aid...But in short space
It rained down fortune show'ring on your head,
And such a flood of greatness fell on you,
What with our help, what with the absent king,
50 What with the injuries of a wanton time,
The seeming sufferances that you had borne,
And the contrarious winds that held the king
So long in his unlucky Irish wars
That all in England did repute him dead:
And from this swarm of fair advantages
You took occasion to be quickly wooed
To gripe the general sway into your hand,
Forgot your oath to us at Doncaster,
And being fed by us you used us so
60 As that ungentle gull, the cuckoo's bird,
Useth the sparrow—did oppress our nest,
Grew by our feeding to so great a bulk
That even our love durst not come near your sight
For fear of swallowing; but with nimble wing
We were enforced for safety sake to fly
Out of your sight and raise this present head,
Whereby we stand opposéd by such means
As you yourself have forged against yourself,
By unkind usage, dangerous countenance,
70 And violation of all faith and troth
Sworn to us in your younger enterprise.
    King. These things indeed you have articulate,
Proclaimed at market-crosses, read in churches,
To face the garment of rebellion
With some fine colour that may please the eye
Of fickle changelings and poor discontents,
Which gape and rub the elbow at the news

Of hurlyburly innovation.
And never yet did insurrection want
Such water-colours to impaint his cause,   80
Nor moody beggars starving for a time
Of pellmell havoc and confusion.
 Prince. In both our armies there is many a soul
Shall pay full dearly for this encounter,
If once they join in trial. Tell your nephew,
The Prince of Wales doth join with all the world
In praise of Henry Percy. By my hopes,
This present enterprise set off his head,
I do not think a braver gentleman,
More active-valiant or more valiant-young,   90
More daring or more bold, is now alive
To grace this latter age with noble deeds.
For my part, I may speak it to my shame,
I have a truant been to chivalry,
And so I hear he doth account me too;
Yet this before my father's majesty—
I am content that he shall take the odds
Of his great name and estimation,
And will, to save the blood on either side,
Try fortune with him in a single fight.   100
 King. And, Prince of Wales, so dare we venture thee,
Albeit considerations infinite
Do make against it...No, good Worcester, no,
We love our people well—even those we love
That are misled upon your cousin's part—
And will they take the offer of our grace,
Both he, and they, and you, yea, every man
Shall be my friend again and I'll be his.
So tell your cousin, and bring me word
What he will do. But if he will not yield,   110
Rebuke and dread correction wait on us,

And they shall do their office. So, be gone;
We will not now be troubled with reply.
We offer fair, take it advisedly.

[Worcester and Vernon go

Prince. It will not be accepted, on my life.
The Douglas and the Hotspur both together
Are confident against the world in arms.

King. Hence, therefore, every leader to his charge,
For on their answer will we set on them,
120 And God befriend us, as our cause is just!

*[they disperse to their commands; Falstaff plucks
the Prince by the sleeve as he turns away*

Falstaff. Hal, if thou see me down in the battle and
bestride me, so, 'tis a point of friendship.

Prince. Nothing but a colossus can do thee that
friendship. Say thy prayers, and farewell.

Falstaff. I would 'twere bed-time, Hal, and all well.

Prince. Why, thou owest God a death.

[he hurries off

Falstaff. 'Tis not due yet, I would be loath to pay him
before his day. What need I be so forward with him
that calls not on me? Well, 'tis no matter, honour pricks
130 me on. Yea, but how if honour prick me off when I
come on? how then? can honour set to a leg? no—or an
arm? no—or take away the grief of a wound? no.
Honour hath no skill in surgery then? no. What is
honour? a word. What is in that word honour? what is
that honour? air. A trim reckoning! Who hath it?
he that died a-Wednesday. Doth he feel it? no. Doth
he hear it? no. 'Tis insensible then? yea, to the dead.
But will it not live with the living? no. Why? Detraction
will not suffer it. Therefore I'll none of it. Honour is
140 a mere scutcheon—and so ends my catechism. *[he goes*

[5. 2.]   *A plain near the rebel camp*

WORCESTER and VERNON approach, returning from the King

Worcester. O, no, my nephew must not know,
    Sir Richard,
The liberal and kind offer of the king.
  Vernon. 'Twere best he did.
  Worcester.   Then are we all undone.
It is not possible, it cannot be,
The king should keep his word in loving us.
He will suspect us still, and find a time
To punish this offence in other faults.
Supposition all our lives shall be stuck full
Of eyes,
For treason is but trusted like the fox,   10
Who, ne'er so tame, so cherished and locked up,
Will have a wild trick of his ancestors.
Look how we can, or sad or merrily,
Interpretation will misquote our looks,
And we shall feed like oxen at a stall,
The better cherished still the nearer death.
My nephew's trespass may be well forgot,
It hath the excuse of youth and heat of blood,
And an adopted name of privilege—
A hare-brained Hotspur, governed by a spleen.   20
All his offences live upon my head
And on his father's. We did train him on,
And his corruption being ta'en from us,
We as the spring of all shall pay for all...
Therefore, good cousin, let not Harry know,
In any case, the offer of the king.
  Vernon. Deliver what you will, I'll say 'tis so.
Here comes your cousin.

*Hotspur and Douglas, with officers
and soldiers come to meet them*

Hotspur. My uncle is returned.
30 Deliver up my Lord of Westmoreland.
Uncle, what news?
   Worcester. The king will bid you battle presently.
   Douglas. Defy him by the Lord of Westmoreland.
   Hotspur. Lord Douglas, go you and tell him so.
   Douglas. Marry, and shall, and very willingly.
                                 [he goes
   Worcester. There is no seeming mercy in the king.
   Hotspur. Did you beg any? God forbid!
   Worcester. I told him gently of our grievances,
Of his oath-breaking—which he mended thus,
40 By now forswearing that he is forsworn.
He calls us rebels, traitors, and will scourge
With haughty arms this hateful name in us.

Douglas returns

   Douglas. Arm, gentlemen, to arms! for I have thrown
A brave defiance in King Henry's teeth,
And Westmoreland that was engaged did bear it,
Which cannot choose but bring him quickly on.
   Worcester. The Prince of Wales stepped forth before
      the king,
And, nephew, challenged you to single fight.
   Hotspur. O, would the quarrel lay upon our heads,
50 And that no man might draw short breath to-day
But I and Harry Monmouth! Tell me, tell me,
How showed his tasking? seemed it in contempt?
   Vernon. No, by my soul. I never in my life
Did hear a challenge urged more modestly,
Unless a brother should a brother dare

To gentle exercise and proof of arms.
He gave you all the duties of a man,
Trimmed up your praises with a princely tongue,
Spoke your deservings like a chronicle,
Making you ever better than his praise   60
By still dispraising praise valued with you,
And, which became him like a prince indeed,
He made a blushing cital of himself,
And chid his truant youth with such a grace,
As if he mast'red there a double spirit
Of teaching and of learning instantly.
There did he pause. But let me tell the world,
If he outlive the envy of this day,
England did never owe so sweet a hope,
So much misconstrued in his wantonness.   70
  Hotspur. Cousin, I think thou art enamouréd
Upon his follies. Never did I hear
Of any prince so wild a liberty.
But be he as he will, yet once ere night
I will embrace him with a soldier's arm,
That he shall shrink under my courtesy.
Arm, arm, with speed—and, fellows, soldiers, friends,
Better consider what you have to do
Than I, that have not well the gift of tongue,
Can lift your blood up with persuasion.   80

A messenger comes up

  Messenger. My lord, here are letters for you.
  Hotspur. I cannot read them now.
O gentlemen, the time of life is short!
To spend that shortness basely were too long,
If life did ride upon a dial's point,
Still ending at the arrival of an hour.
An if we live, we live to tread on kings,

If die, brave death, when princes die with us!
Now, for our consciences, the arms are fair,
90 When the intent of bearing them is just.

Another messenger hurries up

Messenger. My lord, prepare, the king comes
    on apace.
Hotspur. I thank him that he cuts me from my tale,
For I profess not talking—only this,
Let each man do his best. And here draw I
A sword, whose temper I intend to stain
With the best blood that I can meet withal
In the adventure of this perilous day.
Now, Esperance! Percy! and set on.
Sound all the lofty instruments of war,
100 And by that music let us all embrace,
For, heaven to earth, some of us never shall
A second time do such a courtesy.

['*The trumpets sound.*' '*They embrace,*'
and depart in haste to arm

[5. 3.] '*The king enters with his power*' *and marches
past.* '*Alarum to battle. Then enter* DOUGLAS *and* SIR
WALTER BLUNT' (*disguised as the king*) *fighting; they
pause*

Blunt. What is thy name, that in the battle thus
Thou crossest me? what honour dost thou seek
Upon my head?
Douglas.   Know then, my name is Douglas,
And I do haunt thee in the battle thus
Because some tell me that thou art a king.
Blunt. They tell thee true.
Douglas. The Lord of Stafford dear to-day hath bought
Thy likeness, for instead of thee, King Harry,

This sword hath ended him. So shall it thee,
Unless thou yield thee as my prisoner.   10
 Blunt. I was not born a yielder, thou proud Scot,
And thou shalt find a king that will revenge
Lord Stafford's death.

> ['*They fight, Douglas kills Blunt*'

HOTSPUR *comes up*

 Hotspur. O Douglas, hadst thou fought at
        Holmedon thus,
I never had triumphed upon a Scot.
 Douglas. All's done, all's won! here breathless lies
        the king.
 Hotspur. Where?
 Douglas. Here.
 Hotspur. This, Douglas? no, I know this face full well.
A gallant knight he was, his name was Blunt,   20
Semblably furnished like the king himself.
 Douglas. A fool go with thy soul, whither it goes!
A borrowed title hast thou bought too dear.
Why didst thou tell me that thou wert a king?
 Hotspur. The king hath many marching in his coats.
 Douglas. Now, by my sword, I will kill all his coats,
I'll murder all his wardrobe, piece by piece,
Until I meet the king.
 Hotspur.   Up, and away!
Our soldiers stand full fairly for the day.

> [*they rejoin the forces*

'*Alarum. Enter* FALSTAFF, *solus*'

 Falstaff. Though I could 'scape shot-free at London, 30
I fear the shot here, here's no scoring but upon the pate.
Soft! who are you? Sir Walter Blunt—there's honour
for you! here's no vanity! I am as hot as molten lead,

and as heavy too: God keep lead out of me! I need no
more weight than mine own bowels. I have led my
ragamuffins where they are peppered, there's not three
of my hundred and fifty left alive, and they are for the
town's end, to beg during life...But who comes here?

Prince HENRY approaches

Prince. What, stand'st thou idle here? lend me
        thy sword.
40 Many a nobleman lies stark and stiff
Under the hoofs of vaunting enemies,
whose deaths are yet unrevenged. I prithee, lend me
thy sword.
    Falstaff. O Hal, I prithee, give me leave to breathe
awhile. Turk Gregory never did such deeds in arms
as I have done this day.
I have paid Percy, I have made him sure.
    Prince. He is, indeed, and living to kill thee....
I prithee, lend me thy sword.
50 *Falstaff.* Nay, before God, Hal, if Percy be alive,
thou get'st not my sword, but take my pistol if thou wilt.
    Prince. Give it me. What, is it in the case?
    Falstaff. Ay, Hal, 'tis hot, 'tis hot. There's that will
sack a city.
                    [*'The Prince draws it out and finds
                        it to be a bottle of sack'*
    Prince. What, is it a time to jest and dally now?
                    [*' he throws the bottle at him '*, *and goes*
    Falstaff. Well, if Percy be alive, I'll pierce him...
[*aside*] If he do come in my way, so. If he do not, if I
come in his willingly, let him make a carbonado of me.
I like not such grinning honour as Sir Walter hath. Give
60 me life, which if I can save, so; if not, honour comes
unlooked for, and there's an end.   [*he goes*

[5. 4.] '*Alarum, excursions. Enter the* KING, *the* PRINCE', *wounded in the cheek*, 'LORD JOHN *of* LANCASTER, *and* EARL *of* WESTMORELAND'

King. I prithee,
Harry, withdraw thyself, thou bleedest too much.
Lord John of Lancaster, go you with him.
  Lancaster. Not I, my lord, unless I did bleed too.
  Prince. I beseech your majesty, make up,
Lest your retirement do amaze your friends.
  King. I will do so. My Lord of Westmoreland,
lead him to his tent.
  Westmoreland. Come, my lord, I'll lead you to your tent.
  Prince. Lead me, my lord? I do not need your help, 10
And God forbid a shallow scratch should drive
The Prince of Wales from such a field as this,
Where stained nobility lies trodden on,
And rebels' arms triumph in massacres!
  Lancaster. We breathe too long. Come, cousin
            Westmoreland,
Our duty this way lies; for God's sake, come.
            [*Lancaster and Westmoreland hurry forward*
  Prince. By God, thou hast deceived me, Lancaster,
I did not think thee lord of such a spirit.
Before, I loved thee as a brother, John,
But now, I do respect thee as my soul.   20
  King. I saw him hold Lord Percy at the point,
With lustier maintenance than I did look for
Of such an ungrown warrior.
  Prince.   O, this boy
Lends mettle to us all!   [*he follows*

  DOUGLAS *appears from another part of the field*

  Douglas. Another king! they grow like Hydra's heads.
I am the Douglas, fatal to all those

That wear those colours on them. What art thou,
That counterfeit'st the person of a king?

  King. The king himself, who, Douglas, grieves
     at heart

30 So many of his shadows thou hast met,
And not the very king. I have two boys
Seek Percy and thyself about the field,
But seeing thou fall'st on me so luckily
I will assay thee: so, defend thyself.

  Douglas. I fear thou art another counterfeit,
And yet in faith thou bear'st thee like a king,
But mine I am sure thou art, whoe'er thou be,
And thus I win thee.

           ['*They fight. The King being in danger,*
                enter Prince of Wales'

  Prince. Hold up thy head, vile Scot, or thou art like

40 Never to hold it up again! the spirits
Of valiant Shirley, Stafford, Blunt, are in my arms.
It is the Prince of Wales that threatens thee,
Who never promiseth but he means to pay....

                ['*they fight, Douglas flieth*'

Cheerly, my lord, how fares your grace?
Sir Nicholas Gawsey hath for succour sent,
And so hath Clifton—I'll to Clifton straight.

  King. Stay, and breathe awhile.
Thou hast redeemed thy lost opinion,
And showed thou mak'st some tender of my life,

50 In this fair rescue thou hast brought to me.

  Prince. O God! they did me too much injury
That ever said I heark'ned for your death.
If it were so, I might have let alone
The insulting hand of Douglas over you,
Which would have been as speedy in your end
As all the poisonous potions in the world,

And saved the treacherous labour of your son.

 King. Make up to Clifton, I'll to Sir Nicholas Gawsey.

              [he goes

    HOTSPUR *comes up*

 Hotspur. If I mistake not, thou art Harry Monmouth.

 Prince. Thou speak'st as if I would deny my name. 60

 Hotspur. My name is Harry Percy.

 Prince.   Why, then I see

A very valiant rebel of the name.

I am the Prince of Wales, and think not, Percy,

To share with me in glory any more:

Two stars keep not their motion in one sphere,

Nor can one England brook a double reign,

Of Harry Percy and the Prince of Wales.

 Hotspur. Nor shall it, Harry, for the hour is come

To end the one of us, and would to God

Thy name in arms were now as great as mine! 70

 Prince. I'll make it greater ere I part from thee,

And all the budding honours on thy crest

I'll crop, to make a garland for my head.

 Hotspur. I can no longer brook thy vanities.

           ['they fight'

    FALSTAFF *draws near*

 Falstaff. Well said, Hal! to it, Hal! Nay, you shall find no boy's play here, I can tell you.

DOUGLAS *returns;* 'he *fighteth with* FALSTAFF', *who* '*falls down as if he were dead*'; *he passes on.* HOTSPUR *is wounded, and falls.*

 Hotspur. O, Harry, thou hast robbed me of my youth!

I better brook the loss of brittle life

Than those proud titles thou hast won of me.

They wound my thoughts worse than thy sword my flesh. 80

But thought's the slave of life, and life time's fool,
And time that takes survey of all the world
Must have a stop. O, I could prophesy,
But that the earthy and cold hand of death
Lies on my tongue: no, Percy, thou art dust,
And food for—   [*he dies*
  Prince. For worms, brave Percy. Fare thee well,
    great heart!
Ill-weaved ambition, how much art thou shrunk!
When that this body did contain a spirit,
90 A kingdom for it was too small a bound,
But now two paces of the vilest earth
Is room enough. This earth, that bears thee dead,
Bears not alive so stout a gentleman.
If thou wert sensible of courtesy,
I should not make so dear a show of zeal—
But let my favours hide thy mangled face!
    [*he covers Hotspur's eyes with a plume from his helm*
And even in thy behalf I'll thank myself
For doing these fair rites of tenderness.
Adieu, and take thy praise with thee to heaven!
100 Thy ignominy sleep with thee in the grave,
But not remembered in thy epitaph!
        ['*he spieth Falstaff on the ground*'
What! old acquaintance! could not all this flesh
Keep in a little life? poor Jack, farewell!
I could have better spared a better man:
O, I should have a heavy miss of thee,
If I were much in love with vanity:
Death hath not struck so fat a deer to-day,
Though many dearer, in this bloody fray.
Embowelled will I see thee by and by,
110 Till then in blood by noble Percy lie.   [*he goes*
  Falstaff ['*riseth up*']. Embowelled! if thou embowel
me to-day, I'll give you leave to powder me and eat me

too to-morrow. 'Sblood, 'twas time to counterfeit, or
that hot termagant Scot had paid me, scot and lot too.
Counterfeit? I lie, I am no counterfeit. To die is to be
a counterfeit, for he is but the counterfeit of a man, who
hath not the life of a man: but to counterfeit dying, when
a man thereby liveth, is to be no counterfeit, but the
true and perfect image of life indeed. The better part
of valour is discretion, in the which better part I have 120
saved my life. 'Zounds, I am afraid of this gunpowder
Percy, though he be dead. How, if he should counterfeit too, and rise? by my faith, I am afraid he would
prove the better counterfeit. Therefore I'll make him
sure, yea, and I'll swear I killed him. Why may not he
rise as well as I? Nothing confutes me but eyes, and
nobody sees me: therefore, sirrah, [*stabs him*] with a
new wound in your thigh, come you along with me.

[' *he takes up Hotspur on his back* '

The PRINCE and LORD JOHN of LANCASTER return

Prince. Come, brother John, full bravely hast
      thou fleshed
Thy maiden sword.
    Lancaster.   But, soft! whom have we here?   130
Did you not tell me this fat man was dead?
    Prince. I did, I saw him dead,
Breathless and bleeding on the ground. Art thou alive?
Or is it phantasy that plays upon our eyesight?
I prithee, speak. We will not trust our eyes,
Without our ears. Thou art not what thou seem'st.
    Falstaff. No, that's certain, I am not a double-man:
but if I be not Jack Falstaff, then am I a Jack: there is
Percy! [*throws the body down*] If your father will do me
any honour, so; if not, let him kill the next Percy him- 140
self...I look to be either earl or duke, I can assure you.

Prince. Why, Percy I killed myself, and saw thee dead.

Falstaff. Didst thou? Lord, Lord, how this world is given to lying! I grant you I was down and out of breath, and so was he, but we rose both at an instant, and fought a long hour by Shrewsbury clock. If I may be believed, so: if not, let them that should reward valour bear the sin upon their own heads. I'll take it
150 upon my death, I gave him this wound in the thigh. If the man were alive, and would deny it, 'zounds, I would make him eat a piece of my sword.

Lancaster. This is the strangest tale that ever I heard.

Prince. This is the strangest fellow, brother John. Come, bring your luggage nobly on your back.

[*aside, to Falstaff*

For my part, if a lie may do thee grace,
I'll gild it with the happiest terms I have.

['*a retreat is sounded*'

The trumpet sounds retreat, the day is ours.
Come, brother, let's to the highest of the field,
160 To see what friends are living, who are dead.   [*they go*

Falstaff. I'll follow, as they say, for reward. He that rewards me, God reward him! If I do grow great, I'll grow less, for I'll purge, and leave sack, and live cleanly as a nobleman should do.

[*he follows, dragging off the body*

[5. 5.] '*The Trumpets sound. Enter the* KING, PRINCE *of* WALES, LORD JOHN *of* LANCASTER, EARL *of* WEST-MORELAND, *with* WORCESTER *and* VERNON *prisoners*'

King. Thus ever did rebellion find rebuke.
Ill-spirited Worcester! did not we send grace,
Pardon and terms of love to all of you?
And wouldst thou turn our offers contrary?

Misuse the tenour of thy kinsman's trust?
Three knights upon our party slain to-day,
A noble earl and many a creature else,
Had been alive this hour,
If like a Christian thou hadst truly borne
Betwixt our armies true intelligence.   10

 Worcester. What I have done my safety urged me to;
And I embrace this fortune patiently,
Since not to be avoided it falls on me.

 King. Bear Worcester to the death, and Vernon too:
Other offenders we will pause upon.

     [*Worcester and Vernon are led away*
How goes the field?

 Prince. The noble Scot, Lord Douglas, when he saw
The fortune of the day quite turned from him,
The noble Percy slain, and all his men
Upon the foot of fear, fled with the rest,   20
And falling from a hill, he was so bruised
That the pursuers took him. At my tent
The Douglas is; and I beseech your grace
I may dispose of him.

 King.   With all my heart.

 Prince. Then, brother John of Lancaster, to you
This honourable bounty shall belong.
Go to the Douglas, and deliver him
Up to his pleasure, ransomless and free.
His valours shown upon our crests to-day
Have taught us how to cherish such high deeds,   30
Even in the bosom of our adversaries.

 Lancaster. I thank your grace for this high courtesy,
Which I shall give away immediately.

 King. Then this remains, that we divide our power.
You, son John, and my cousin Westmoreland
Towards York shall bend, you with your dearest speed

To meet Northumberland and the prelate Scroop,
Who, as we hear, are busily in arms:
Myself and you, son Harry, will towards Wales,
40 To fight with Glendower and the Earl of March.
Rebellion in this land shall lose his sway,
Meeting the check of such another day,
And since this business so fair is done,
Let us not leave till all our own be won.   [*they go*

GLOSSARY

Note. Where a pun or quibble is intended, the meanings are distinguished as (*a*) and (*b*)

ADMIRAL, flagship; 3. 3. 25

ADVANTAGE, 'at more advantage' = at a more favourable opportunity; 2. 4. 533

ADVERTISEMENT, (i) news; 3. 2. 172, (ii) counsel; 4. 1. 36

ADVISEDLY, 'take advisedly' = consider carefully; 5. 1. 114

AFFECTIONS, inclinations. Often in a bad sense (cf. *Lucr.* 500; *2 Hen. IV*, G.); 3. 2. 30

AGATE-RING, ring with seal cut in agate (cf. *Rom.* 1. 4. 55); 2. 4. 69

ALARUM (or ALARM) to battle. From O.Fr. 'alarme' (= to arms), but erroneously interpreted = 'all arm!'; 5 3 1 (S.D.), 30 (S.D.), 5. 4. 1 (S.D.)

AMAZE, dismay, perplex; 2. 4. 77 (S.D.); 5. 4. 6

ANCIENT, ensign-bearer, flag; 4. 2. 23, 30

ANGEL, gold coin = 10*s*.; 4. 2. 6

ANSWER (vb.), discharge, defend, guarantee; 1. 3. 185; 3. 3. 175; 4. 2. 8

ANTIC, ridiculously old-fashioned person; 1. 2. 60

APPLE-JOHN. Ripened about St John's Day (midsummer), and was eaten two years later when shrivelled and wrinkled; 3. 3. 4

APPOINTMENT, detail of dress; 1. 2. 168

APPROVE, put to the test; 1. 1. 54; 4. 1. 9

ARBITREMENT, scrutiny; 4. 1. 70

ARGUMENT, theme; 2. 2. 93; 2. 4. 277

ART, science, magic; 3. 1. 47

ARTICULATE, set out in articles, tabulate; 5. 1. 72

ASPECT, (*a*) respect, (*b*) Astrol. position of one heavenly body in relation to another; 1. 1. 97

ATTEMPT, escapade; 3. 2. 13

ATTRIBUTION, credit, honour; 4. 1. 3

AUDITOR, royal official who examined the accounts of receivers, sheriffs, etc. (Minshew); 2. 1. 56

BACON, (*a*) bumpkin, (*b*) fat man; 2. 2. 89

BAFFLE, degrade (a knight) by hanging him up by the heels (cf. note 2. 4. 428–9, *Ric. II*, G., and Spenser, *F.Q.* vi, vii. 27); 1. 2. 99

BAITED. Lit. 'refreshed as at an inn' (cf. note and *Euphues*, Bond i, 323, 'A pleasant companion is a bayte in a journey'); 4. 1. 99

BALKED, (*a*) ploughed in ridges, (*b*) defeated; 1. 1. 69

BAND, bond, debt; 3. 2. 157

BARE, (i) beggarly; 3. 2. 13; (ii) (a) thread-bare, (b) lean; 4. 2. 67–9, (iii) patent; 1. 3. 108

BASE-STRING, lowest note; 2. 4. 5–6

BASILISK, largest type of cannon, called after the fabulous reptile (cf. *culverin*); 2. 3. 55

BASTARD, a common Sp. wine, brown or white; 2. 4. 26, 72

BASTINADO, cudgelling. Sp. 'bastonada'; 2. 4. 332

BATE, diminish in weight or number or energy; 3. 3. 2; 4. 3. 26

BATTLE, battle-array; 4. 1. 129

BAVIN. Lit. fire-wood; 3. 2. 61

BEAR, convey meaning; 4. 1. 20

BEAR (a point), take up a fencing position; 2. 4. 192

BEAR HARD, resent; 1. 3. 267

BEAST, fool, idiot (O.E.D. 5); 3. 3. 123

BEAVER. Lit. part of helmet guarding mouth and chin; 4. 1. 104

BEEF, fat ox; 'sweet beef' = unsalted beef; 3. 3. 176

BELDAM, grandam (disrespectful); 3. 1. 31

BIRD, chick; 5. 1. 60

BLOOD, spirit, vigour; 3. 1. 179; 4. 3. 76

BLOWN, inflated; 4. 2. 47

BLUE-CAPS, blue bonnets. A term of contempt for Scots. Lit. 'servants' (who wore blue caps in England); 2. 4. 352

BOLTER, cloth for sifting flour from bran; 3. 3. 70

BOLTING-HUTCH, bakers' branbin (v. *bolter*); 2. 4. 441–2

BOMBARD, large leather vessel to hold liquor; 2. 4. 443

BOMBAST, padding (for clothes); 2. 4. 323

BOOK, legal document; 3. 1. 221, 263

BOOTS, booty (a quibble); 2. 1. 81; 3. 1. 66

BOTS, worms. A horse disease; 2. 1. 9

BOW-CASE, i.e. for a fiddler's bows; 2. 4. 245

BRACH, bitch-hound; 3. 1. 235

BRAVE, fine, glorious; 1. 1. 53; 1. 2. 63; 5. 2. 88

BRAWN, fatted boar-pig; 2. 4. 107

BREAK WITH, tell, reveal to; 3. 1. 142

BREATHE, (i) utter; 1. 1. 3; (ii) pause; 1. 3. 102; 2. 4. 15, 246; 5. 4. 15

BRIEF, letter; 4. 4. 1

BRING ON, bring out; 1. 3. 275

BRISK, smartly dressed; 1. 3. 54

BRUISE, crush (cf. *Meas.* 2. 1. 5–6); 3. 2. 105

BUFFETS, 'go to buffets' = fall to blows; 2. 3. 33

BULL'S-PIZZLE, bull's penis, 'formerly a much-used instrument of flagellation' (O.E.D.); 2. 4. 243

BUSKY, bushy; 5. 1. 2

BY-DRINKING, drink between meals; 3. 3. 74

BY-ROOM, side-room; 2. 4. 28

CADDIS, worsted tape, used for cheap garters; 2. 4. 69

CALIVER, light musket; 4. 2. 19

CALL ON, demand payment from; 5. 1. 129

CAMBYSES (son of Cyrus), K. of Persia 529–522 B.C.; 2. 4. 381

CAMOMILE, creeping plant, often covering the paths of Eliz. gardens; 2. 4. 395

CANKER, (i) wild rose (with quibble on ii), (ii) ulcer; 1. 3. 176; 4. 2. 29

CANK'RED, malignant; 1. 3. 137

CANSTICK, candlestick; 3. 1. 129

CANTLE, 'projecting corner of land' (O.E.D.); 3. 1. 98

CAPITULATE, draw up articles of agreement; 3. 2. 120

CARBONADO, rasher; 5. 3. 58

CARD, adulterate (esp. of drink); 3. 2. 62

CARRY AWAY, transport (figur.); 2. 3. 77

CASE (sb.), suit of clothes; 1. 2. 172

CASE (vb.), cover the face or body; 2. 2. 51

CAST, a throw at dice; 4. 1. 47

CATERPILLAR, blood-sucker (cf. *Ric. II*, 2. 3. 166); 2. 2. 83

CESS. Aphetic f. 'assess'; 'out of all cess' = beyond computation; 2. 1. 7

CHAMBER-LYE, urine; 2. 1. 20

CHAMBERLAIN, bedroom attendant (cf. *Macb.* 1. 7. 63); 2. 1. 46, 49

CHANGELING, renegade; 5. 1. 76

CHARGE, (i) valuables; 2. 1. 45, 57; (ii) cost; 3. 1. 110, 113; (iii) military command; 1. 1. 35; 2. 4. 536; 3. 2. 161; 4. 2. 23; 5. 1. 118; (iv) mandate; 4. 3. 41

CHARLES' WAIN, the Great Bear. Orig. Charlemagne's Wain; 2. 1. 2

CHEAP (sb.), v. *good cheap*; 3. 3. 44–5

CHEWET, jackdaw, chatter-box; 5. 1. 29

CHIMNEY, fireplace; 2. 1. 20

CHOPS, or CHAPS, (*a*) fat cheeks, (*b*) butcher's 'chops'; 1. 2. 131

CHUFF, close-fisted churl (cf. Nashe, p. 192); 2. 2. 88

CITAL, summons (cf. *Hen. VIII*, 4. 1. 29); 5. 2. 63

CLEANLY, deft; 2. 4. 447

CLIPPED IN, embraced; 3. 1. 43

CLOAK-BAG, portmanteau; 2. 4. 440

CLOSE (sb.), encounter. Fencing term; 1. 1. 13

CLOSE (adj. and adv.), hidden, secret; 2. 2. 3, 74, 95; 2. 3. 112; 2. 4. 530

CLOUDY, gloomy (cf. *Macb.* 3. 6. 41); 3. 2. 83

COAT, coat-armour, i.e. 'a vest of rich material embroidered with heraldic devices worn ...over armour' (O.E.D.); 4. 1. 100; 5. 3. 25, 26

COCK-SURE, with perfect safety; 2. 1. 85

COLOUR (sb.), pretext, semblance; 3. 2. 100; 5. 1. 75, 80

COLOUR (vb.), disguise; 1. 3. 109

COLT (vb.), (*a*) befool, (*b*) mount (cf. *Cymb.* 2. 4. 133); 2. 2. 36–7

COME AWAY, come along. Still colloq. in Scotland; 2. 1. 22, 23

COME ON, enter the field; 5. 1. 131

COMFORT, succour; 4. 1. 56

COMMAND, authority; 4. 4. 32

COMMODITY, lit. packet of goods upon which money could be raised at the usurers (v. *Meas.* G.); 1. 2. 82; 4. 2. 17

COMMON-HACKNEYED, vulgarised, prostituted; 3. 2. 40

COMMUNITY, over-familiarity; 3. 2. 77

COMPARATIVE, abusive, personal (cf. *L.L.L.* 5. 2. 840); 1. 2. 79; (as sb.) 3. 2. 67

COMPASS, (*a*) moderation; 3. 3. 19, 20; (*b*) circumference; 3. 3. 22, 23

CONCEALMENT, secret art; 3. 1. 165

CONDITION, disposition; 1. 3. 6

CONFEDERACY, conspiracy; 4. 4. 38

CONFOUND, consume; 1. 3. 100

CONJUNCTION, joint force; 4. 1. 37

CONTAGIOUS, pestilential; 1. 2. 190

CONTINENT, river bank; 3. 1. 108

CORINTHIAN, gay dog, 'wencher' (Johnson); 2. 4. 11

CORRIVAL, partner; 1. 3. 207; 4. 4. 31

COURSE, phase; 3. 1. 41

COZEN (vb.), cheat; 1. 2. 119

COZENER (sb.), cheat; 1. 3. 254

CRANK (vb.), wind, double (cf. *V.A.* 682); 3. 1. 96

CRESSET. Lit. an iron basket upon a pole in which pitched rope, etc. was burnt for illumination, e.g. of playhouses (v. Cotgrave, 'Falot'); 3. 1. 14

CRISP, curling; 1. 3. 106

CRY OUT UPON, denounce (cf. *A.Y.L.* 2. 7. 70); 4. 3. 81

CULVERIN, small cannon (from Fr. *couleuvrin* = adderlike); 2. 3. 55

CURRENT (sb.), vicissitude; 2. 3. 57

CURRENT (adj.), accepted as true or fashionable; 1. 3. 68; 2. 1. 53; 2. 3. 96

CUSHES, armour for the thighs; 4. 1. 105

CUT, short for 'curtal', a horse with docked tail; 2. 1. 5

DAFF, stand aside from, ignore. A variant of 'doff'; 4. 1. 96

DARE, daring; 4. 1. 78

DAY, 'by the day' = o'clock; 2. 1. 1

DEAR, precious, estimable, heartfelt; 1. 1. 33; 4. 1. 34; 4. 4. 31; 5. 4. 95

DEAREST, utmost, direst; 3. 1. 180; 3. 2. 123; 5. 5. 36

DEEP (v. note); 3. 1. 52

DEFY, renounce, despise; 1. 3. 228; 4. 1. 6

DENIER. Fr. coin = $\frac{1}{12}$ of a sou; 3. 3. 80

DENY, (i) refuse; 1. 3. 25, 29, 77; (ii) refuse to admit; (quibble) 2. 4. 485

DEPUTATION, 'by d.' = through substitutes; 4. 1. 32; 'in d.' = as viceregents; 4. 3. 87

DEPUTY, or 'Deputy of the Ward', who acted as magistrate in the absence of an alderman; 3. 3. 116

DETERMINATION, mind; 4. 3. 33

DIRECTLY, without evasion; 2. 3. 88

DISDAINED, disdainful; 1. 3. 183

DISLIKE, discord; 5. 1. 26

DISPUTATION, conversation; 3. 1. 203

DITTY, the words of a song; 3. 1. 122, 206

DIVISION. Musical term = melodic passage; 3. 1. 208

DOUBLE-MAN, wraith (v. O.E.D. 'double' adj. C. 2c, sb. 2c); 5. 4. 137

DOWLAS, coarse linen; 3. 3. 69

DRAFF, pig-wash; 4. 2. 34

DRAWER, tapster; 2. 4. 7, etc.

GLOSSARY

DRAWN FOX i.e. false trail; 3. 3. 114

DRENCH, dose (for a horse); 2. 4. 104

DURANCE, (a) stout cloth; (b) imprisonment; 1. 2. 43

DUTY, due; 5. 2. 57

DYE SCARLET, drink deep; 2. 4. 14–15

EMBOSSED, (a) swollen, (b) at bay; 3. 3. 156

EMBOWEL, disembowel (a) a corpse for embalming, (b) a deer after the kill; 5. 4. 109, 111

ENFEOFF, sell with absolute possession; 3. 2. 69

ENGAGE, give as a hostage; 4. 3. 95; 5. 2. 45

ENGROSS UP. Lit. buy up wholesale; 3. 2. 148

ENLARGEMENT, release from confinement; 3. 1. 30

ENVY (sb.), ill-will; 1. 3. 27; 5. 2. 68

ENVY (vb.), begrudge; 4. 3. 35

ESSENTIALLY MADE, i.e. gold by nature; 2. 4. 482

ESTRIDGE, ostrich. The usual Eliz. meaning 4. 1. 98

EXHALATION, exhaled meteor (q.v.); 2. 4. 316

EXHALED METEOR, comet, meteor (q.v.) supposedly engendered from vapours drawn up by the sun (cf. Rom. 3. 5. 13); 5. 1. 19

EXPEDIENCE, enterprise; 1.1. 33

EXPEDITION, progress; 4. 3. 19

EXTREMITY, severity; 1. 2. 181

FACE, trim (v. guard); 5. 1. 74

FALL OFF, revolt; 1. 3. 94

FAT, 'Of a room: full of dense air' (O.E.D.); hence— stuffy; 2. 4. 1

FAT-WITTED, dull (cf. L.L.L. 5. 2. 268, and Chapman, Ovid's Banquet, st. 115, 'fat and foggy brains'); 1. 2. 3

FAVOUR, (i) feature; 3. 2. 136; (ii) token or badge worn in the helmet; 5. 4. 96

FAZE or FEAZE, fray, wear thin; 4. 2. 30

FEAR (vb.), fear for; 4. 1. 24; 4. 2. 56

FEELING (adj.), affecting; 3. 1. 203

FIDDLE-STICK, 'the devil rides upon a fiddlestick'=what a fuss about a trifle!; 2. 4. 477

FINE, refined, subtle; 4. 1. 2

FINGER. A measure = ¾ inch; 4. 2. 72

FLESH (vb.), blood (cf. 2 Hen. IV, 4. 5. 132); 5. 4. 129

FOOL, plaything (cf. Rom. 3. 1. 141; Son. 116. 9); 5. 4. 81

FOOT-LAND-RAKER, foot-pad (rake = roam); 2. 1. 72

FORM, 'the essential principle' (O.E.D.); 1. 3. 210

FORSWEAR, (i) swear to abandon; 2. 2. 15; (ii) (a) deny on oath, (b) swear falsely; 5. 2. 40

FORWARD, (a) eager, (b) premature; 5. 1. 128

FRANKLIN, 'landowner of free but not noble birth' (O.E.D.); 2. 1. 54

FRETFUL, (a) given to worry, (b) wearing away; 3. 3. 11

FRONTIER, (i) frontier fortress (cf. Ham. 4. 4. 16); 1. 3. 19; (ii) rampart, 2. 3. 54

FUBBED or FOBBED, cheated; 1. 2. 59

FURNISHED, equipped (horse and man); 4. 1. 97; 5. 3. 21

FURNITURE, military equipment; 3. 3. 200

GIB CAT, tom cat (Gib = Gilbert); 1. 2. 73

GILD, give specious lustre to; 5. 4. 157

GOD DEFEND, God forbid; 4. 3. 38

GOD SAVE THE MARK! 'Prob. orig. a formula to arrest an evil omen, whence used in way of apology when something horrible, disgusting, indecent or profane had been mentioned' (O.E.D.). Here expresses impatient scorn; 1. 3. 56

GOD'S ME = God save me; 2. 3. 96

GOLDEN, auspicious, flattering (cf. *A.Y.L.* 1. 1. 6); 4. 3. 73

GOOD CHEAP, bon marché, cheap; 3. 3. 44–5

GORBELLIED, pot-bellied; 2. 2. 87

GOVERNMENT, (i) conduct, self-control (cf. *3 Hen. VI*, 1. 4. 132); 1. 2. 27; 3. 1. 182; (ii) military command; 4. 1. 19

GRACE, 'do g. to' = bring credit to; 2. 1. 70; 5. 4. 156 (with quibble on 'grace' = salvation)

GRIEF, (i) bodily pain; 1. 3. 51; 5. 1. 132; (ii) grievance; 4. 3. 42, 48

GRIFFIN. Fabulous animal, with eagle's head, forelegs and wings, and lion's body, hind legs and tail; 3. 1. 150

GUARD, ornamental band or border, different in colour and material from the rest of the garment; unfashionable by end of 16th c. (Linthicum); 3. 1. 256

GULL, unfledged nestling; 5. 1. 60

GUMMED, stiffened with gum; 2. 2. 2

GURNET, gurnard, marine fish of genus *Trigla* (v. note); 4. 2. 12

GUTS, (i) belly, intestines, (ii) butcher's offal, (iii) skin for sausages and black puddings, (iv) greed, gluttony, (v) a corpulent or gluttonous person; 2. 4. 224, 255, 443; 3. 3. 152, 155

HA?, eh? 1. 1. 75; 1. 3. 278

HABITS, clothes; 1. 2. 168

HAIR. 'Of one hair' = of one colour and appearance, hence 'hair' came to mean 'sort, kind, character' (O.E.D.); 4. 1. 61

HALF-FACED. Lit. as of a face on a coin, hence = thin, wretched, half-and-half (cf. *K. John*, 1. 1. 92); 1. 3. 208

HAPPY MAN BE HIS DOLE. Prov. phrase for wishing good luck (Apperson, p. 284). Lit. may his lot ('dole') be that of a happy man; 2. 2. 75

HARDIMENT, prowess; 1. 3. 101

HARLOTRY (adj. and sb.), 'A term of playful contempt, without any thought of the origin of the word' (Clar.); 2. 4. 389; 3. 1. 197

HARNESS, armour; 3. 2. 101

HAZARD, (a) a game at dice (v. *Sh. Eng.* ii. 470), (b) chance; 4. 1. 48

HEAD, (i) current driven against a bank; 1. 3. 106; (ii) armed force; 1. 3. 281; 3. 2. 102, 167; 4. 3. 103; 4. 4. 25; 5. 1. 66. Cf. *make head*

HEADY, impetuous; 2. 3. 57

HEARKEN FOR, wait or long for (cf. *Shrew*, 1. 2. 250); 5. 4. 52

HEART!, by God's heart!; 3. 1. 247

HEART (out of), (a) dispirited, (b) in poor condition; 3. 3. 6

HEAVY, ominous, grievous; 2. 3. 65; 5. 4. 105 (quibble)

HEST. Meaning doubtful (v. note); 2. 3. 64

HOLD IN, keep counsel; 2. 1. 76

HOLD LEVEL, claim equality; 3. 2. 17

HOLD PACE, keep up, rival; 3. 1. 48

HOLD WELL, be apt; 1. 2. 30

HOLD A WING, keep a course; 3. 2. 30

HOLIDAY (adj.), gay, dainty (cf. *Wives*, 3. 2. 62; 'festival' *Ado*, 5. 2. 40); 1. 3. 46

HOLLAND, fine quality linen, first made in Holland; 3. 3. 72

HOLY-ROOD DAY, Sept. 14th; 1. 1. 52

HOPE, (i) expectation; 1. 2. 203; (ii) promise; 3. 2. 36

HOSE, trunk hose (mod. 'breeches'); 2. 4. 212

HUMOROUS, moody, odd; 3. 1. 230

HUMOUR, (i) physiol. the four fluids of the human body (here, in an excessive quan-tity); 2. 4. 441; (ii) inclination, fancy, mood; 1. 2. 69, 188; 2. 4. 91; 3. 1. 170

IMPAWN, give as a hostage; 4. 3. 108

INCOMPREHENSIBLE, infinite; 1. 2. 178

INDENT (sb.), indentation; 3. 1. 102

INDENT (vb.), enter into a formal agreement; 1. 3. 87

INDENTURE, sealed agreement (made in duplicate with indented edges that fit together); 2. 4. 46; 3. 1. 78, 139, 260

INDIRECT, (a) not directly derived, (b) crooked, unjust; 4. 3. 105

INDIRECTLY, off-hand, evasively; 1. 3. 66

INDUCTION, first steps; 3. 1. 2

INJURY, (i) insult; 3. 3. 161; (ii) evil; 5. 1. 50

INNOVATION, rebellion (the usual sense in Sh.); 5. 1. 78

INSENSIBLE, not to be seen or felt; 5. 1. 137

INSTANTLY, simultaneously; 5. 2. 66

INSULTING, scornfully triumphant; 5. 4. 54

INTELLIGENCE, espionage; 4. 3. 98

INTEMPERATURE, (a) 'distempered condition of the body' (O.E.D.), (b) unbridled licentiousness; 3. 2. 156

INTEND, purpose to travel; 4. 1. 92

INTERCEPT, interrupt; 1. 3. 151

INTEREST, title; 3. 2. 98

INWARD, internal; 1. 3. 58; 4. 1. 31

IRON, pitiless (cf. *2 Hen. IV*,
4. 2. 8); 2. 3. 50

ITERATION, the repetition of
the Scriptures etc. in worship (cf. Hooker, *Ecc. Pol.*
bk. 5, xxxvii. 2, 'why we
iterate the Psalms'); 1.2.89

JACK, (i) knave. A term of contempt; 2. 4. 11; 3. 3. 86,
138; 5. 4. 138; (ii) a sleeve-
less jacket 'formerly worn
by foot-soldiers...usually of
leather quilted' (O.E.D.);
4. 2. 47

JOINED-STOOL, stool made by
a joiner. Often the subject
of some obscure jest now
lost; 2. 4. 374

JORDAN, chamber-pot; 2. 1. 19

JUMP WITH, agree with; 1.2.68

JUSTLING, jostling; 4. 1. 18

KEEP, dwell; 1. 3. 244

KENDAL GREEN, coarse green
cloth, in 16th c. only worn
by labourers, but perhaps
traditionally associated with
Robin Hood; 2. 4. 219

KNOTTY-PATED, block-headed;
2. 4. 224

LAY BY, stand and deliver.
Orig. doubtful; 1. 2. 35

LAY OUT, disburse; 4. 2. 5

LAY THE PLOT, organize, direct;
2. 1. 51

LEADEN DAGGER. A theatrical
property, 'type of ineffectual
weapon' (O.E.D.); 2. 4. 375

LEAPING-HOUSE, brothel; 1. 2. 9

LEASH, set of three (dogs);
2. 4. 6

LEG (sb.), bow; 2. 4. 379

LET SLIP, unleash; 1. 3. 277

LEWD, vile; 3. 2. 13

LIBERTY, licence (cf. *Meas.*
1. 3. 29); 5. 2. 73

LIE, assume a fencing posture;
2. 4. 192

LIKING, (*a*) inclination, (*b*) good
bodily condition; 3. 3. 5

LIMIT, (i) 'limits of the
charge' = distribution of
commands in an army; 1. 1.
35; (ii) division, district;
3. 1. 71; (iii) prescribed
bounds (of allegiance); 4.
3. 39

LINE (sb.), degree, category.
Lit. series; 1. 3. 168; 3. 2. 85

LINE (vb.), reinforce; 2. 3. 85

LIQUOR, v. note; 2. 1. 84

LIST, extremity; 4. 1. 51

LIVE, lie, exist; 1. 2. 182; 4.
1. 56; 5. 2. 21

LIVERY, v. *sue his livery*; 4. 3.
62

LOACH, small fresh-water fish;
2. 1. 21

LOOK BIG, threaten; 4. 1. 58

LOOP, loop-hole (e.g. in a castle-
wall); 4. 1. 71

LOOSE GOWN or 'loose-bodied
gown'. Hung, without
waist, from neck to foot,
'so that any deformity, however monstrous, remains
hidden' (Linthicum, 183);
3. 3. 3

LUGGED, baited (of bears or
bulls); 1. 2. 73

MAID MARIAN, v. note; 3. 3.
115

MAIN, (*a*) army, (*b*) stake
at 'hazard' (q.v.); 4. 1. 47

MAINLY, nightily; 2. 4. 197

MAINTENANCE, bearing; 5. 4.
22

MAJORITY, pre-eminence; 3.
2. 109

MAKE UP, move forward; 5. 4. 5, 58

MALT-WORM, drunkard; lit. weevil that breeds in malt; 2. 1. 74

MAMMET, doll, puppet; orig. 'mawmet' (Mahomet) = idol; 2. 3. 94

MANAGE, horsemanship; 2. 3. 51

MANNER (with the), in the act. From 'mainour' = stolen property found upon a thief at arrest; 2. 4. 311

MANNINGTREE, Essex town 'famous for the revelry indulged in at its fairs, and for the fatness of its oxen' (Clar.); 2. 4. 444

MARK, 13s. 4d. or two nobles. A sum of money, not a coin; 2. 1. 55; 2. 4. 511; 3. 3. 42, 83

MASTER, possess (cf. *Son.* 106. 8); 5. 2. 65

MATCH (sb.), plot, device; 2. 4. 88; 'set a match', lit. make an appointment, (in thieves' cant) arrange a meeting between highwaymen and victims; 1. 2. 104

MATCH (vb.), join, associate; 1. 1. 49; 3. 2. 15

MEAN, instrument; 1. 3. 260

MEDICINE, drug (of any kind); 2. 2. 18

MELT, take pity on (cf. *2 Hen. IV*, 4. 4. 32); 2. 4. 117

MEMENTO MORI, ring with a death's head; 3. 3. 30–1

METEOR, atmospheric phenomenon of any kind, e.g. 'airy' = wind, 'watery' = rain, snow, etc., 'fiery' = lightning, shooting stars, etc. (cf. *Errors*, 4. 2. 6 and G.); 1. 1. 10; 2. 4. 316; 5. 1. 19

METTLE, natural vigour; 2. 4. 12, 344; 4. 3. 22; 5. 4. 24

MICHER, truant; 2. 4. 402

MIDRIFF, diaphragm; 3. 3. 155

MILLINER, dealer in gloves, bands, etc., which were perfumed to make them more marketable. Orig. 'of Milan'; 1. 3. 36

MINCE, walk with affected delicacy; 3. 1. 132

MINION, darling, favourite; 1. 1. 83; 1. 2. 26

MISPRISION, mistake; 1. 3. 27

MISQUOTE, misread; 5. 2. 14

MISTREADING, going astray; 3. 2. 11

MISUSE (sb.), abuse; 1. 1. 43, (vb.) misrepresent; 5. 5. 5

MO, more; 4. 4. 31

MOIETY, share; 3. 1. 94

MOLDWARP, mole; 3. 1. 147

MOOR-DITCH, section of old city moat, draining the fen of Moorfields, seldom if ever cleaned out; 1. 2. 77

MORE AND LESS, high and low; 4. 3. 68

MOUTHED, gaping; 1. 3. 97

MOVE, urge, appeal to; 2. 3. 33

MUDDY, filthy (O.E.D. 7); 2. 1. 96

MUSTER (take a), call troops together; 4. 1. 133

MUTUAL, shared in common; 1. 1. 14

NAKED, desolate; 4. 3. 77

NEAT (adj.), spruce; 1. 3. 33

NEAT (sb.), ox; 2. 4. 243

NECK, 'in the n. of' = following directly upon. A race-course expression (cf. *Son.* 131. 11); 4. 3. 92

NETHERSTOCKS, stockings; 2. 4. 112–13

New-fall'n, recently acquired; 5. 1. 44

Not-pated, close-cropped; 2. 4. 69

Offer, offer battle (cf. 3. 2. 169); 4. 1. 69

Old lad of the castle, roisterer or wencher (cf. G. Harvey, ed. Grosart, i. 225, ii. 44; and Nashe, ed. McKerrow, iii. 5, l. 18); 1. 2. 42

Omnipotent, almighty (jocular; cf. Nashe, p. 191); 1. 2. 107

Onyer, ? clerk to Exchequer (v. note); 2. 1. 75

Opinion, (i) arrogance; 3. 1. 183, (ii) public opinion (cf. Oth. 1. 3. 225); 3. 2. 42; (iii) reputation; 4. 1. 77; 5. 4. 48

Out-face, bluff, browbeat; 2. 4. 253

Owe, own; 5. 2. 69

Painted cloth, cheap wall-hanging (cf. 2 Hen. IV, G. 'waterwork'); 4. 2. 25

Parcel, (i) detail, item; 2. 4. 98; 3. 2. 159; (ii) set, lot (contemptuous); 2. 4. 442

Participation, fellowship; 3. 2. 87

Passage, action (cf. Tw.Nt. 3. 2. 70); 3. 2. 8

Passion, grief, pain; 2. 4. 380, 410; 3. 1. 34

Pay, settle, kill; 2. 4. 189, 215; 5. 3. 47; 5. 4. 43, 114

Pay home, deal effectively with; 1. 3. 285

Pepper, make it hot for; 2. 4. 188

Pepper-gingerbread, a cheap

kind made with pepper instead of ginger; 3. 1. 255

Phantasy, hallucination; 5. 4. 134

Pickthank, obsequious tale-bearer; 3. 2. 25

Pinch, worry; 1. 3. 229; 3. 1. 28

Pismires, ants; 1. 3. 240

Play off, toss off (a bumper); 2. 4. 16

Pocket up, swallow (an insult); 3. 3. 162

Point, (i) pommel of saddle; 2. 1. 6; (ii) (a) sword-point, (b) one of the tagged laces suspending the hose from the doublet; 2. 4. 211

Policy, craft in public affairs; 1. 3. 108

Politician, intriguer; 1. 3. 241

Pomgarnet, pomegranate; 2. 4. 37

Popinjay, parrot, chattering overdressed coxcomb; 1. 3. 50

Popularity, keeping company with common people; 3. 2. 69

Portly, stately; 1. 3. 13

Possessed, informed; 4. 1. 40

Post (sb.), courier; 1. 1. 37

Post (vb.), travel express; 5. 1. 35

Poulter, poulterer; 2. 4. 429

Pouncet-box, small perfume-box with perforated lid; 1. 3. 38

Powder (vb.), salt for pickling; 5. 4. 112

Power, army; 1. 1. 22, et passim

Precedent (v. note); 2. 4. 32

Predicament, category, lit. that which is predicated (logic); 1. 3. 168

PRICK (vb.), (a) spur; (b) finish off, lit. tick off (by pricking a hole on a list; cf. *Jul. Caes.* 4. 1. 1–3); 5. 1. 129–30

PRIDE, (i) height; 1. 1. 60; (ii) mettle; 4. 3. 22

PRIVILEGE, (i) pre-eminence; 3. 2. 86; (ii) 'of privilege' = which confers immunity; 5. 2. 19

PROFITED, proficient; 3. 1. 164

PROPORTION, size; 4. 4. 15

PRUNE, preen; 1. 1. 98

PUDDING, stuffing for a roast; 2. 4. 444

PUKE-STOCKINGS, cheap stockings made of dyed cloth; 2. 4. 69

PUNY, novice; 2. 4. 29

PUPIL AGE, minority (orig. 'pupil' = minor); 2. 4. 92

PURCHASE, (i) plunder (cant); 2. 1. 91; (ii) purchasing power; 3. 3. 40

PURGE, (i) clear; 3. 2. 20; (ii) amend one's life, (b) take aperient; 5. 4. 163

PUSH (stand the), become the butt of; 3. 2. 66

QUALITY, party; 4. 3. 36

QUESTION (sb.), discussion; 1. 1. 34; (vb.) talk with; 1. 3. 47

QUIDDITY, subtle jest (cf. *Ham.* 5. 1. 96); 1. 2. 45

RABBIT-SUCKER, sucking rabbit; 2. 4. 429

RASCAL, (a) scoundrel, (b) lean deer; 3. 3. 157

RASH, quickly inflammable; 3. 2. 61

RAZE or Race, root of ginger; 2. 1. 24

READ, (i) act as tutor; 3. 1. 45; (ii) learn, discover; 4. 1. 49

REBUKE, violent check; 5. 5. 1

REMOVED, not directly concerned; 4. 1. 35

RENDEZVOUS, refuge (cf. *Hen. V*, 2. 1. 18; 5. 1. 88); 4. 1. 57

REPRISAL, prize, lit. prize at sea; 4. 1. 118

REPROOF, disproof; 1. 2. 182; 3. 2. 23

REWARD, portions of the deer thrown to the hounds at the end of a chase (v. note); 5. 4. 161

RIOT, wantonness; 1. 1. 85

RIVO. A toper's exclamation of doubtful meaning; Arden cf. *Jew of Malta*, 4. 6. 10, '*Rivo Castiliano*', which it translates 'Castilian stream', i.e. liquor; 2. 4. 108

ROUNDLY, plainly; 1. 2. 22

ROYAL, coin worth 10s.; 1. 2. 136

SACK, v. note; 1. 2. 3–4, *et passim*

SAD, serious; 1. 1. 56

SAINT NICHOLAS' CLERKS, v. note; 2. 1. 60

SARCENET, soft thin silk material (fig.); 3. 1. 251

SAVING YOUR REVERENCE. An apology for mentioning something unpleasant; 2. 4. 460

SCANDALIZED, disgraced; 1. 3. 154

SCHOOLED, admonished; 3. 1. 188

SCORE (vb.), (i) chalk up a reckoning; 2. 4. 26, (ii) make cuts or notches (with quibble on i); 5. 3. 31

SCOT (v. note); 1. 3. 214

SCOT AND LOT, full and final payment; 5. 4. 114

SCUTCHEON or escutcheon, shield or hatchment of arms painted on wood and used at funerals; 5. 1. 140

SEASON, age, period; 4. 1. 4

SECOND, subordinate (v. *2 Hen. IV*, G.); 1. 3. 165

SEMBLABLY, in like fashion; 5. 3. 21

SENSIBLE, capable of feeling; 5. 4. 94

SERVE, suffice for; 4. 1. 132

SET (vb.), stake; 4. 1. 46, 47

SET OFF (his head), not reckoned (to his account); 5. 1. 88

SET TO, set (a limb); 5. 1. 131

SETTER, 'one employed by robbers...to spy upon their intended victims' (O.E.D.); 2. 2. 49

SHAPE, conception, conjecture; 1. 1. 58

SHAVE, (a) fleece, (b) have the head shaved; 3. 3. 59

SHOT, (a) payment for drink, (b) i.e. from a gun; 5. 3. 30–1

SHOTTEN, (of a herring) that has shed its roe, (hence) emaciated, good-for-nothing; 2. 4. 126

SHRINK, shiver (cf. *A.Y.L.* 2. 1. 9); 5. 2. 76

SKIMBLE-SKAMBLE, scamped together anyhow; 3. 1. 152

SKIPPING, flighty; 3. 2. 60

SMUG, smooth, trim; 3. 1. 100

SNEAK-UP, a mean, creeping scoundrel; 3. 3. 86

SNUFF (take in), (a) snuff up and sneeze, (b) take umbrage at; 1. 3. 41

So, good! very well!; 5. 1. 122; 5. 3. 57, 60

SOFT, wait a bit!; 1. 3. 155; 2. 1. 35; 5. 4. 130

SOOTHER, flatterer; 4. 1. 7

SOUSED, pickled in salt; 4. 2. 12

SPANISH POUCH, cheap pouch of Spanish leather; 2. 4. 70

SPEAR-GRASS or spear wort; 2. 4. 305–6

SPLEEN, supposed the organ of sudden action or impulse, (hence) irritability, caprice, ill-humour, impetuosity; 2. 3. 80; 3. 2. 125; 5. 2. 20

SPOIL (sb.), ruin; 3. 3. 10

SQUIER, foot-ru e; 2. 2. 12

STAMP, mintage, begetting; 4. 1. 4

STAND FOR, (a) be good for, (b) represent; 1. 2. 136

STANDING, gone stiff (v. note); 2. 4. 245

START, sudden fit; 3. 2. 125

STARTING-HOLE, bolt-hole (for a hunted animal); 2. 4. 260

STARVE, die of cold; 1. 3. 159; 2. 2. 20

STATE, (i) state-chair, throne; 2. 4. 372, 374; (ii) dignity; 3. 2. 62; (iii) kingdom, estate, fortune; 3. 2. 98, 169; 4. 1. 46

STEWED PRUNE, bawd (because a brothel commonly displayed a dish of prunes in the window); 3. 3. 114

STIR, be up and about (cf. *Jul. Caes.* 2. 2. 110); 3. 2. 46

STOCK-FISH, dried cod or ling; 2. 4. 243

STOMACH, appetite; 2. 3. 43

STORE, capital, savings; 2. 2. 88

STRAPPADO, torture by disjointing the limbs; 2. 4. 234

STRIKER, foot-pad (cf. Ger. *Landstreicher*); 2. 1. 73

STUDY, pursuit; 1. 3. 228

SUBMISSION, confession; 3. 2. 28

SUDDENLY, soon; 1. 3. 291

SUE A LIVERY, make legal claim for delivery of land; 4. 3. 62

SUFFERANCE, suffering; 5. 1. 51

SUGGESTION, instigation; 4. 3. 51

SUPPLY, reinforcements; 4. 3. 3

SURE. (a) harmless' (b) safe; 5. 3. 47; 5. 4. 125–6

SURVEY, oversight, control (O.E.D. 2); 5. 4. 82

TAFFETA, light lustrous silk fabric; 1. 2. 11

TALL, doughty; 1. 3. 62

TALLOW, animal fat of any kind, dripping from a roast (cf. *Errors*, 3. 2. 98); 2. 4. 108

TALLOW-CATCH, dripping-pan (?); 2. 4. 225

TARGET, buckler; 2. 4. 199

TASK, (i) challenge; 4. 1. 9; 5. 2. 52, (ii) tax; 4. 3. 92

TASTE, test; 4. 1. 119

TEMPER, brightness (cf. *Ric. II*, 4. 1. 29); 5. 2. 95

TEMPT, try; 3. 1. 172

TENDER (make tender of), have regard for; 5. 4, 49

TERMAGANT, imaginary Mo—hammedan deity of turbulent character, belonging to morality plays; 5. 4. 114

THEREFORE, for that purpose; 1. 1. 30

THICK, dim; 2. 3. 48

TICKLE-BRAIN, strong liquor (slang); 2. 4. 391–2

TILT, contend. Often used equivocally; 2. 3. 94

TIME, (i) time of life, life; 3. 2. 36, 151; (ii) affairs; 4. 1. 25

TOO BLAME, too blameworthy. A 16th and 17th c. mis-understanding of the infin.

'to blame' used predicatively (O.E.D. 'blame' vb. 6); 3. 1. 175

TOASTS-AND-BUTTER, milksop. Lit. eater of buttered toast; 4. 2. 20

TOSSED, vexed; 2. 3. 81

TOUCH, touchstone, 'bide the touch' = stand the test; 4. 4. 10

TOWN'S END, outskirt of town or village, where rubbish was shot, stocks stood and beggars congregated (v. quots. O.E.D.); 4. 2. 9; 5. 3. 38

TRACE, follow; 3. 1. 47

TRADE-FALLEN, out of work; 4. 2. 28

TRAIN, entice; 5. 2. 22

TRICK, trait; 2. 4. 398; 5. 2. 12

TRIM (sb.), trappings; 4. 1. 113

TRIM (adj.), fine, pretty (ironical); 5. 1. 135

TRIM UP, deck out; 5. 2. 58

TRIMLY, elegantly; 1. 3. 33

TRIUMPH, torchlight procession; 3. 3. 40

TROJAN, boon companion (cf. *L.L.L.* 5. 2. 674); 2. 1. 68

TRUE, honest; 1. 2. 107; 2. 1. 91; 2. 2. 22, 91; 2. 4. 307

TUCK, long narrow rapier; 2. 4. 245

TURK, ferocious person; 5. 3. 45

UNDER-SKINKER, under-drawer; 2. 4. 23

UNEVEN, untoward; 1. 1. 50

UNGRACIOUS, graceless; 2. 4. 437

UNSORTED, ill-chosen; 2. 3. 14

UNYOKED, uncurbed; 1. 2. 188

VALUED, taken into consideration; 3. 2. 177

VASSAL (adj.), base; 3. 2. 124

VELVET-GUARDS, wearers of velvet trimmings (v. *guard*); 3. 1. 256

VICE, buffoon clad as a fool and armed with a wooden dagger (v. Chambers, *Med. Stage*, ii. 203–5); 2. 4. 445

VIGILANT, wakeful; 4. 2. 56

VIZARD, visor, mask; 1. 2. 123, 171; 2. 2. 51

WAG, naughty boy. Often a term of endearment; 1. 2. 16, 23, 44; 4. 2. 48

WAIT, attend upon; 5. 1. 111

WANTON, (i) luxuriant; 3. 1. 211; (ii) sportive; 4. 1. 103; (iii) unruly; 5. 1. 50

WARM, well-to-do (O.E.D. 8); 4. 2. 17

WASP-STUNG, irritable; 1. 3. 236

WATERING, the act of drinking; 2. 4. 15

WELL-RESPECTED, well-considered; 4. 3. 10

WELL SAID!, bravo! well done!; 5. 4. 75

WELSH, gibberish (a quibble); 3. 1. 49, 118

WELSH HOOK, woodman's bill-hook; 2. 4. 334

WILD (sb.), weald; 2. 1. 54

WILD (adj.), (*a*) untamed, insubordinate; 5. 2. 12; (*b*) dissolute; 5. 2. 73

WILDFIRE, (*a*) highly inflammable preparation of gunpowder, (*b*) erysipelas; 3. 3. 39

WIND, wheel; 4. 1. 109

WORSHIP, honour; 3. 2. 151

WRING, gall; 2. 1. 6

WRITER, notary; 3. 1. 141

YOUNKER, prodigal son. Lit. 'younger' (brother); 3. 3. 80

ZEAL, loyalty, affection; 4. 3. 63; 5. 4. 95

WORDSWORTH CLASSICS

General Editors: Marcus Clapham and Clive Reynard
Titles in this series

DISTRIBUTION

**AUSTRALIA, BRUNEI
& MALAYSIA
Reed Editions**
22 Salmon Street, Port Melbourne
Vic 3207, Australia
Tel: (03) 646 6716
Fax (03) 646 6925

**DENMARK
BOG-FAN**
St. Kongensgade 61A
1264 København K

BOGPA SIKA
Industrivej 1, 7120 Vejle Ø

**FRANCE
Bookking International**
16 Rue des Grands Augustins
75006 Paris

**GERMANY, AUSTRIA
& SWITZERLAND
Swan Buch-Marketing GmbH**
Goldscheuerstrabe 16
D-7640 Kehl Am Rhein, Germany

**GREAT BRITAIN & IRELAND
Wordsworth Editions Ltd**
Cumberland House, Crib Street,
Ware, Hertfordshire SG12 9ET

Selecta Books
The Selectabook
Distribution Centre
Folly Road, Roundway, Devizes
Wiltshire SN10 2HR

**HOLLAND & BELGIUM
Uitgeverlj en Boekhandel**
Van Gennep BV, Spuistraat 283
1012 VR Amsterdam, Holland

**INDIA
OM Book Service**
1690 First Floor
Nai Sarak, Delhi – 110006
Tel: 3279823-3265303 Fax: 3278091

**ITALY
Magis Books**
Piazza Della Vittoria l/C
42100 Reggio Emilia
Tel: 0522-452303 Fax: 0522-452845

**NEW ZEALAND
Whitcoulls Limited**
Private Bag 92098, Auckland

**NORWAY
Norsk Bokimport AS**
Bertrand Narvesensvei 2
Postboks 6219, Etterstad, 0602 Oslo

**PORTUGAL
Cashkeen Limited**
(Isabel Leao) 25 Elmhurst Avenue
London N2 0LT
Tel: 081- 444 3781 Fax: 081- 444 3171

**SINGAPORE
Book Station**
18 Leo Drive, Singapore
Tel: 4511998 Fax: 4529188

**SOUTH EAST CYPRUS
Tinkerbell Books**
19 Dimitri Hamatsou Street, Paralimni
Famagusta, Cyprus
Tel: 03-8200 75

**SOUTH WEST CYPRUS & GREECE
Huckleberry Trading**
4 Isabella, Anavargos, Pafos, Cyprus
Tel: 06-231313

**SOUTH AFRICA, ZIMBABWE
CENTRAL & E. AFRICA
Trade Winds Press (Pty) Ltd**
P O Box 20194, Durban North 4016

**SPAIN
Ribera Libros**
Dr. Areilza No.19, 48011 Bilbao
Tel: 441-87-87 Fax: 441-80-29

**USA, CANADA & MEXICO
Universal Sales & Marketing**
230 Fifth Avenue, Suite 1212
New York, N Y 10001 USA
Tel: 212-481-3500 Fax: 212-481-3534

**DIRECT MAIL
Redvers**
Redvers House, 13 Fairmile,
Henley-on-Thames, Oxfordshire RG9 2JR
Tel: 0491 572656 Fax: 0491 573590